FAULKNER AND OE

The Self-Critical Imagination

Akio Kimura

D1563675

University Press of America,® Inc.
Lanham · Boulder · New York · Toronto · Plymouth, UK

Copyright © 2007 by
University Press of America,® Inc.
4501 Forbes Boulevard
Suite 200
Lanham, Maryland 20706
UPA Acquisitions Department (301) 459-3366

Estover Road
Plymouth PL6 7PY
United Kingdom

Library of Congress Control Number: 2006937931
ISBN-13: 978-0-7618-3663-6 (paperback : alk. paper)
ISBN-10: 0-7618-3663-2 (paperback : alk. paper)

Contents

Preface

It has always seemed to me that we talk too much about literary influences between two writers: between Confucius and Pound, between *Bhagavad-Gita* and Thoreau, between Radiguet and Mishima, between Faulkner and Oe, etc. As I read Faulkner through Oe and Oe through Faulkner for this study, however, I began to think that there was nothing—no such thing as link, connection, transition, or translation—between Faulkner and Oe, even though I still had to refer to such thing just for convenience. Faulkner wrote in English. Oe wrote in Japanese. From the beginning, how could I expect a literary influence between two writers writing in two different languages? To me, Faulkner is still a strange writer, as strange as Oe, simply because their languages are different from mine. Yes, I am Japanese. But that doesn't mean that Oe's Japanese is the same as mine. I have never felt comfortable reading Oe's Japanese.

This book is about a literal influence rather than a literary influence. In the following pages, we will detect some traces of Faulkner's language in Oe's language, that is, traces of Faulkner's literal influence on Oe. Among those traces, the most confusing for us is that of Faulkner's "*is*" in Oe's self-awareness or his recurrent first-person narrator, "I." Oe metaphorically translates Faulkner's "*is*" into various characters, and finally turns it into a female or hermaphroditic "I." This also concerns Oe's sense of time. Eula's words "You just are" represent a crisis in Oe's male sense of time, or his sense of immortality. Oe's self-awareness as male or authoritarian presence both in Japanese society and in his own family is thus shaken up.

It is well known, perhaps too well known among Japanese Faulkner scholars that Faulkner influenced Oe. I was influenced by such scholarly knowledge about Faulkner's influence on Oe, which had originated in Oe's own remarks on his debt to Faulkner. Like the flue, "Faulkner's influence on Oe" has spread ever since Oe admitted to his debt to Faulkner. However, Oe's use of Faulkner's "*is*" involves much more than what we simply call influence, since Oe himself seems to be more interested in the scenes of failed influence than in those of success. In those scenes of failure, language always stands in between: Gavin's romantic language fails to influence Eula and Linda; Nancy's religious language fails to influence Temple; the old general's cynical language fails to influence the corporal. Under the influence of Faulkner, Oe also created scenes of failed influence. Then did Oe really tell us about "Faulkner's influence on Oe"?

Akio Kimura
Tokyo
June 2006

Acknowledgments

This study was originally a Ph.D. thesis written at Drew University. I thank Merrill Skaggs, Joseph Urgo, and Yasuko Grosjean, for their encouragements, suggestions, and advice. I also thank the Caspersen Scholarship for making this study possible. I thank my wife, Masae, for her support.

Introduction

I

William Faulkner (1897–1962) is a novelist. So is Oe Kenzaburo (1935–), [1] a Japanese novelist who won the 1994 Nobel Prize for literature. In Japanese, the word for novel is *shosetsu*, and novelist *shosetsuka*. Usually, we—even Japanese scholars—do not distinguish between the two. Masao Miyoshi, Japanese scholar of English, Japanese, and Comparative literature teaching at the University of California, San Diego, and a friend of Oe, however, stresses the generic difference between the novel of the West and the Japanese *shosetsu*:

> Genres, like most other things, are specific to history and geography. The *shosetsu* could be viewed as a confluence of narrative possibilities available to Edo and later writers whose perceptions and responses, dreams and realizations, were guided and defined by the constraints of their times. Just as the Western novel developed from an ensemble of epic, Renaissance drama, folklore, and ballad, so the *shosetsu* ranges over the *monogatari* and *utamonogatari*, *noh*, *nikki* and *tabinikki*, Buddhist sermons, *renga*, *kabuki*, and *kana zoshi*. (28)

Combining those legacies from the classic Japanese literature with the influence of the imported Western novels, the *shosetsu* appears in the late 19th century. Although such a generic difference has become nowadays unnoticeable, one aspect of the *shosetsu* still keeps bothering even those who are most nonchalant about the difference: the notorious first-person narrator "I" of the *shosetsu*, especially of the *shishosetsu* (I-fiction).

Referring to Roland Barthes, who says in *Writing Degree Zero* that "the 'he' is a typical novelistic convention" (qtd. in Miyoshi 22), Miyoshi distinguishes between the soliloquy of the novel and the "I" of the *shosetsu*:

> The third person is a mask the Western novel dons almost without exception. The convention demands the distance of the "he" (*sic*) from the author. As the "he" and the author gradually work up to be the third person, the "soliloquy becomes a novel" [qtd. from Barthes].
>
> Against such a victory of the "he/she" over the "I" in the novel, the defeat of the "he/she" at the hands of the "I" characterizes the *shosetsu*. The *shosetsu* is so overwhelmingly marked by the dominance of the "I" form that the *shishosetsu* (I-fiction) is the orthodox convention. (22–23)

The "I" may seem to be a literary convention which the Japanese *shosetsuka* acquired by absorbing the Western individualism. But that is true only on its surface. It is true that Western individualism came into Japan, but it never took root. On the contrary, individualism, egoism, subjectivity, the self were suppressed in Japanese society, and only left their combined image in the "I" of the *shishosetsu*. Since it is only an image, or an imitation, the "I" of the *shishosetsu*, or the *shosetsu* in general, does not share with its Western sources the context in which it came into being. On the contrary, it has become a mere reflection of the Japanese social or cultural climate. Miyoshi explains:

> it is true that the first person is predominant in the *shosetsu*:
> the orthodoxy of Japanese fiction is "I-fiction" that records
> the life of the author. And yet, paradoxically, it is not
> egocentric. Quite unlike the autobiographical novel (wheth-
> er in first or third person) such as *David Copperfield, The
> House of the Dead,* or *Sons and Lovers* that fashions a
> critically selected persona, the *shishosetsu* is a form of
> documentary chronology that supposedly exemplifies the
> normative life of a member of the collective. The writer can
> be eccentric, but in his or her difference the reader merely
> sees the limits of homogeneity. Supposedly, I-fiction is
> always honest and factual, and it rejects fictionality and
> mediation. (48)

Even now, the "I"s of many of Japanese *shosetsu* are the products not
so much of the critical distance between the writer and the society, as
of the sense of simply being there. The only difference—if only we
dare to call it a difference—in this so-called postmodern age is that,
in the growth of consumer society, as Miyoshi puts it, "as a consumer,
the "I" is even less distinguished from the others" (25).

Oe criticizes such a persistent "I" of the Japanese *shosetsu*.
Especially, as we will see, Oe's feminist turn in the 1980s is
concerned with the criticism of the male "I" in his own novels. In his
1991 conversation with Donald Pease and Rob Wilson, published as
"A Conversation with Oe Kenzaburo" in *boundary 2* in 1993, Oe
called his own first-person male narrator "I" an "*idée fixe*" and spoke
of an urgent need to "relativize" it with a new narrative technique
(23). This conversation well indicates Oe's awareness of his being
split between the sense of "I" which he inherited from the Japanese
shosetsu, and the idea of "I" which he learned from the Western
novels. Oe is a writer who is always motivated or even haunted by the
need to "relativize" or criticize his presence in his work. That makes

him a rare novelist in Japan. After the revision of "I" in the 1980s through a feminist turn, Oe finally finds in the 1990s a hermaphroditic narrator or focal character who can "relativize" his seeming presence as the male "I" in his previous work.

Although several Japanese writers are said to be influenced by Faulkner, Oe has gained most worldwide attention through the Nobel Prize. Along with Nakagami Kenji (1946–1992), Oe has published a series of novels which features such characteristics as a fictional place based on the writer's own native village or region, characters who suffer from sins committed by their fathers or grandfathers, and a multilayered narrative structure—that is, characteristics attributed to Faulkner's Yoknapatawpha saga. The problem is that the Faulkner who is linked to Oe and Nakagami is always the originator of Yoknapatawpha novels—in particular, *The Sound and the Fury* and *Absalom, Absalom!* So far, we have failed to acknowledge the influence of Faulkner's other works on those writers. This is especially the case with Oe, whose novels reflect more literary influences and perfect more subtle narrative techniques. Generally speaking, literary influence on Oe has not been studied full-scale even in Japan. As to Faulkner's influence, critical attention has centered on the comparison between *The Sound and the Fury* or *Absalom, Absalom!* and *Man'en gannen no futtoboru* (trans. as *The Silent Cry*, 1967).[2] The aim of the present study is not only to expand the lists of books to be compared between Faulkner and Oe, but also to show the Faulknerian influence in Oe's satirical or self-critical imagination—especially on his feminist or hermaphroditic criticism of male "I"—, which is represented especially in Oe's novels written after 1980.

II

Oe was born in 1935 in a small village called Ose located in Shikoku, the smallest of four major islands which form Japan. He was ten years old when World War II ended; he saw the adult Japanese around him listen with deep sorrow to the Emperor's thin voice telling his people through the radio that the war was over. After the war, educated in the new school system, Oe became an avid advocate of democracy, though not necessarily agreeing with Japan's postwar politics led somewhat dictatorially by the Liberal Democratic Party. The post-World War II Japan outwardly followed the American democracy and commercialism, but at the same time inwardly maintained its centripetal tendency and the feudalistic morals. Rather than pretending to look at this situation as an objective outsider, Oe has taken upon himself to criticize Japan's double bind situation from within himself. Oe knows both sides too well. Oe was born too early to avoid the influence of the Emperor-centered ideology of imperial Japan before and during World War II; at the same time he was born too late to advocate a new totalitarian Japan after the war, as thinly disguised by a democratic constitution, with the Emperor as its symbolic center.[3]

Such in-between character, which Oe himself referred to as the "ambiguous" in his Nobel Prize speech, characterizes his point of view. Oe stresses the ambiguity between values split between before and after World War II; the sense of Japanese identity versus the sense of guilt toward the surrounding countries or victimized people abused by Japanese militarism; sympathy with the discarded in Japan's cultural or political margins versus ambition for his own success in Tokyo; the "traditional Japanese sense of beauty and sensitivity to nature" ("Japan, the Ambiguous, and Myself" 123) versus his own "spiritual affinity" (114) for his favorite novelists and poets of the West. These contrasts and tensions appeared early in Oe, and typically reflected Japan's situation after World War II. As Stephen Snyder and Philip Gabriel aptly summarize, indeed "in Oe's evocation of the margins—Shikoku, Hiroshima and the *hibakusha* [victims of an atomic air raid], Okinawa, the handicapped—we have, in essence, an opposition based on privileging the margins over the center, an inversion that tends to reify difference over a previously reified center" (7). Such an "opposition," however, has become possible only through Oe's self-criticism, a critical eye directed toward his own, seemingly built-in ambiguity.

Curiously enough, however, as in Snyder and Gabriel's sentence quoted above, all have neglected Oe's "evocation" of those margins that include the feminine. This is inexplicable when we look at a series of Oe's attempts in the 1980s to rebuild his narrative style by absorbing the feminine in various aspects: hence my emphasis on Oe's feminist turn in the 1980s in Chapter Two of the present study. The general neglect of Oe's feminism is related to the general inattention to the influence of Faulkner's feminism, especially that expressed in his later novels, on Oe. It is again inexplicable when we hear Oe say that he reread all of Faulkner's novels—not *The Sound and the Fury* and *Absalom, Absalom!* alone—in English when he was preparing for writing *The Silent Cry* (Oe and Subaru Henshuubu 77), and also that he read the Snopes trilogy intensively when he wrote "Mizukara waga namida o nugui tamau hi" (trans. as "The Day He Himself Shall Wipe My Tears Away," 1971) (Oe and Subaru Henshuubu 196). Moreover, we have to recall here that Oe's 1981 speech on Faulkner included in McHaney (1985) is mainly concerned with the representation of Eula and Linda Snopes in the Snopes trilogy.

Such a neglect of the influence of Faulkner's feminism or of his later novels on Oe, however, is due in part to the fact that the study of Faulkner's feminism itself has not fully developed until the 1980s, that is, until Fowler and Abadie (1986), Gwin (1990), Roberts (1994), Clarke (1994), and Kartiganer and Abadie (1996) appear. And it is also due to the fact that, in spite of such book-length studies as Butterworth (1983) on *A Fable*, Urgo (1989) on the Snopes trilogy and *A Fable*, Polk (1981) on *Requiem for a Nun*, Faulkner's later novels are often regarded as minor, compared with such canonized novels as *The Sound and the Fury*, *As I Lay Dying*, *Light in August*, *Absalom, Absalom!* and *Go Down, Moses*.

It is well known that, in his early days as writer, Oe was most influenced by the American contemporary novelists who were active in the 1950s and the 60s, most notably by Norman Mailer and James

Baldwin. These two may have been more important to him than Jean-Paul Sartre, on whom Oe wrote a graduation thesis for Tokyo University, and under whose influence he published his first short story "Kimyona shigoto" (An Odd Job) in 1957 while still attending the university. Faulkner's later novels belong to this period, and, in this sense, Oe is contemporary to the later Faulkner. Oe's affinity for American literature is rooted in the general feelings of the late 1950s and the 1960s, that is, skepticism, rebellion, and liberation of the oppressed (minority, women) and the repressed (sex, drugs). Oe's interest in Faulkner, especially in the later Faulkner, is also embedded in this atmosphere.

As Oe himself suggests, Faulkner provided him with models for writing at two important points in his career: one was when he wrote *The Silent Cry*, and the other was when he wrote *"Ame no ki" o kiku onnatachi* (Women Who Listen to the "Rain Tree," 1982).[4] On the one hand, beginning with *The Silent Cry*, Oe wrote a series of novels in which a fictional place, or a microcosm, like his native village appears, the obvious equivalent of Faulkner's Yoknapatawpha novels. On the other hand, beginning with *"Ame no ki" o kiku onnatachi*, and yet more fully in two novels written in the later 1980s, *Jinsei no shinseki* (trans. as *An Echo of Heaven*, 1989) and *Shizukana seikatsu* (trans. as *A Quiet Life*, 1990), Oe used the feminine as a means to caricature his first-person male narrator, Oe's persona. That persona misrepresents the female characters—Gavin Stevens (mis)represents Eula and Linda in *The Town* and *The Mansion*, and also Temple Stevens in *Requiem for a Nun*.

Combined complexly, the coupled borrowings from Faulkner—Yoknapatawpha, as well as the feminine—bring forth in the 1990s two monumental works, *Moeagaru midori no ki: sanbusaku* (A Flaming Green Tree: Trilogy, 1993, 1994, 1995) and *Chugaeri* (trans. as *Somersault*, 1999). At this point we notice the third moment in which Oe comes closest to Faulkner. Oe depicts two successive religious movements in the fictional native village through the eyes of a hermaphrodite or homosexual narrator or focal character. Oe then criticizes the situation in which the religious pursuit of immortality paradoxically incurs the apocalyptic pursuit of the end of the world—the situation which, especially in *Somersault*, is likened to Japan's situation at World War II in which the Emperor's or the authoritarian male's immortality leads to Hiroshima and Nagasaki, that symbolize the end of the world. This is especially Faulknerian once we realize that in *A Fable* the old general is a hermaphrodite, and through his eyes Faulkner reveals the irony in which the pursuit of man's—male—immortality through fighting wars only leads to the wholesale destruction of humankind.

Three chapters of the present study deal with these three moments in which Oe meets Faulkner. Throughout, we will see how Faulkner's idea of "*is*" appears in both Faulkner's and Oe's texts we read. The sense of time expressed in "*is*," or the notion of human heart which holds such a sense of time, links Faulkner to Oe most powerfully. Though disguised in other ideas and expressed by various characters, "*is*" represents both in Faulkner and Oe the feminine or the hermaphrodite which criticizes the masculine represented by the idea of immortality and also, though paradoxically, by its flip side, the idea of the end of the world.

In the first chapter, we will see how Oe metaphorically translates Faulkner's "*is*" into various characters and ideas, and uses it as the binding motif throughout the series of novels in which he creates his own Yoknapatawpha-like literary microcosm. Such metaphors include *Kowasuhito* (the Destroyer) in *Dojidai gemu* (The Game of Contemporaneity, 1979), *mori no fushigi* (the wonder of the forest) in *M/T to mori no fushigi no monogatari* (M/T and the Story of the Wonder of the Forest, 1986), *natsukashii toshi* (the year of nostalgia) in *Natsukashii toshi e no tegami* (Letters to the Year of Nostalgia, 1987), and the idea of leap in *The Silent Cry*. In this context, special attention will be paid to the first two short stories of *"Ame no ki" o kiku onnatachi*, in which, as he metaphorically translates Faulkner's "*is*" into the idea of grief, or its collateral image of *ame no ki* or the "rain tree," Oe explores the function of metaphors in his writings. The chapter also includes a discussion on the political implication of Oe's metaphorical rendering of Faulkner's "*is*." By juxtaposing his own Yoknapatawpha with Japan, Oe reveals the metaphoricity, or even fictionality, of Japan's immortality which is metaphorically rendered by the Emperor's eternal presence. Oe's curious suggestion of the connection between "The Day He Himself Shall Wipe My Tears Away" and the Snopes trilogy is concerned with the criticism of such a metaphorical rendering of immortality or the eternal presence in Japanese politics and culture.

Chapter Two discusses how reading Faulkner, especially the later novels, affects Oe's feminist turn in the 1980s. Throughout the 1980s, to maintain a critical difference between the Emperor-centered Japan and his own Yoknapatawpha, Oe engages in a revision of the male-centeredness of his literary microcosm. Especially, Oe's target is his own habitual first-person male narration, which is the equivalent of the authoritarian presence of the Emperor in Japan. We see here another, but most important, Faulknerian influence on Oe. In his 1981 speech on Faulkner, Oe pays a special attention to the distance which Gavin Stevens keeps between himself and Eula or Linda Snopes in *The Town* and *The Mansion*. We will see how such a distance through which Gavin turns both Eula and Linda, who represent "*is*," into his favorite image of "*was*," is applied by Oe in his 1989 novel *An Echo of Heaven*. It becomes the distance which the narrator-novelist "I" keeps between himself and his friend-heroine Marie, and through which "I" tries to turn her into a Virgin Mary. Marie, however, slips out of "I"'s narrative, and, like Eula and Linda, frustrates "I"'s imagination.

Oe's criticism of his own male first-person narrator "I" continues in his next novel *A Quiet Life*. In Chapter Two, we will also see a parallel between *A Quiet Life* and Faulkner's *Requiem for a Nun*, in terms of the criticism of the tyranny of the subject-object relationship, or the monologic—or male—language which inhabits such a relationship, through the feminine. In *Requiem for a Nun*, influenced by Gavin's and Nancy's languages, Temple is locked into the subject-object relationship. Temple's skepticism or her "*is*," however, keeps resisting such a lock-in. We will see a similar situation in Oe's *A Quiet Life*, in which Ma-chan critically imitates her father's, or Oe's, narrative language—especially its first-person male narration—by, like Derrida's deconstruction, revealing its dependence on her—feminine—doubling or quotation. Ma-chan's female "I" deconstructs the authoritarian presence of the male "I."

Oe's feminist turn in the 1980s bears its fruit in the 1990s in the form of the hermaphrodite narrator or focal character in the Flaming Green Tree trilogy and *Somersault*, both of which, so far, culminate Oe's own Yoknapatawpha novels. In Chapter Three, we see in *Somersault* the opposition between Patron's idea of time as fluidity and Guide's idea of time that ends, which corresponds to the Faulknerian opposition between "*is*" and "*was*." We will also compare *Somersault* with Faulkner's *A Fable*, and see how in both novels the male idea of time that ends, or the end of the world, is criticized from the viewpoint of the feminine or the hermaphrodite. As we have seen above, the idea of time that ends, or the end of the world, is the flip side of the sense of male immortality which prevails in the Emperor-centered Japan. In *Somersault*, Ikuo's hermaphroditism provides the reader with the viewpoint which sees through such a masculine sense of time which connects immortality to the end of the world, and opposes to Faulkner's "*is*." In *A Fable*, the old general's hermaphroditism represents such a viewpoint which is split between "*is*," the corporal, and the world-ending war, which is paradoxically supported by the idea of *man*'s immortality.

Notes

1. I am writing the Japanese names as Japanese do, that is, surname first, regarding them as proper nouns. However, for convenience, the critics' or the scholars' names are written as they appeared in their books or articles.
2. See Ohashi (1984), Kimura (1991) and Fujihira (1999).

3. In discussing Oe's treatment of the Emperor's authoritarian presence, or centrality, in Japanese society, I had in mind Yamaguchi Masao's analyses of the Japanese emperor system, for example, his 1976 essay "Tennosei no shochoteki kukan" (The Symbolic Space of the Emperor System). It is well known that Yamaguchi's structuralist anthropology influenced Oe. What is described in my present study as the Emperor's centrality, therefore, is symbolic, or metaphorical. It is a metaphor for the male-, father-, and *was*-centered structure of Japan.

4. In the original, the title of the book is: 「雨 の 木」を聴く女たち. *Ame no ki* 雨の木 is always accompanied by *rein tsurii* レイン・ツリー(rain tree) written in *katakana* in ruby, so it should be pronounced as *rein tsurii*. In this study, however, I call the book *"Ame no ki" o kiku onnatachi,* for 雨 の 木 is still to be read as *ame no ki* visually.

Chapter One

A Yoknapatawpha of Oe's Own

From Pun to Metaphor

In the postscript for a reprint of "Mizukara waga namida o nugui tamau hi" ("The Day He Himself Shall Wipe My Tears Away"), written twenty years after the publication of the novella, Oe reveals his debt to Faulkner: "Before I wrote this novella, I had been intensively reading Faulkner for four or five years. I think that my understanding of especially the Snopes trilogy style has borne its fruit here, as if it poured itself out" (my translation); 僕はこの小説を書く四、五年ほど前からフォークナーを集中的に読んでいましたが、とくに「スノープス三部作」の文体の 自分なりの読みとりの成果が、自然に流露するような仕方でここにあらわれていると思います ("Shonen no tamashii ni kokuin sareta" 267). This revelation comes as a kind of surprise for readers, even for those who have already known that Oe intensively read Faulkner in preparation for *Man'en gannen no futtoboru* (*The Silent Cry*). The novella does not seem to have anything in common with Faulkner's novels—especially not the Snopes trilogy.

We know Oe likes to talk about every kind of book he reads. As to Faulkner, he even points out differences between Joseph Blotner's

and David Minter's biographical treatments of Faulkner's affair with
Joan Williams (*Shosetsu no takurami, chi no tanoshimi* 51). But we
wonder why he would say nothing about *Requiem for a Nun* or *A
Fable*, both of which, as we shall see in the following chapters, show
rather an obvious relevance to some of his writings. However, before
puzzling over Oe's references to Faulknerian sources, we need to
consider whether our focus is too shallow or too deep. Faulkner can
probably be found anywhere in Oe, even in his everyday attitudes
toward family, friends, readers, and himself; Faulkner's influence
merges in Oe's novels and short stories with motifs, settings,
characters through style, vocabulary, and even wordplay.

   In several essays, Oe expresses his partiality for a Faulknerian
term "grief."[1] Although Oe has written several novels and short
stories using the motif of grief, *"Ame no ki" o kiku onnatachi*, among
others, is a text that Oe "wrote with the word *hitan*, or grief, placed at
the heart of the images of central characters" (my translation); 悲嘆と
いう言葉を、中心にある登場人物のイメージの核心において・・・書
きました (*Shosetsu no takurami, chi no tanoshimi* 154). There, Oe
draws a kind of pun out of the word "grief." In Japanese, grief can be
translated as *kanashimi, hitan, hiai, aware*, etc. In "'Ame no ki' o
kiku onnatachi," the title short story of the volume, Oe presents a
person named Takayasu Katchan, who has attended the lectures by
Faulkner at the University of Virginia. At his death, his wife, called
Penny, who is not Japanese, expresses in her letter a feeling of grief,
using Japanese word—though written in capitalized alphabet—
"AWARE," which Takayasu has taught her as a translation of the
word grief. Written that way, grief looks to readers' eyes as the
English word "aware," and also connotes *mono no aware*—literally,
sensitivity to things or to the pathos of things—which is quite a
popular idea for most of Japanese readers. Oe seems to be referring to
Murasaki-shikibu's *Genji monogatari* (*The Tale of Genji*, c. 1021),
and also to Kobayashi Hideo's *Motoori Norinaga* (1977, 1982), a
famous study of the eighteenth century thinker, Motoori Norinaga,
who explicates the idea of *mono no aware* in *The Tale of Genji*.

Motoori Norinaga is one of Oe's favorite books and Kobayashi one of
his literary mentors. In *Motoori Norinaga*, Kobayashi points out that
Motoori sees in *mono no aware* not merely a feeling, but rather the
way the human heart keeps moving:

> よろずの事にふれて、おのずから心が感<ウゴ>くという、習
> い覚えた知識や分別には歯が立たぬ、基本的な人間経
> 験があるという事が、先ず宣長には固く信じられてい
> る。心というものの有りようは、人々が「わが心」と
> 気楽に考えている心より深いのであり、それが、事に
> ふれて感<ウゴ>く、事に直接に、親密に感<ウゴ>く、その充実した、
> 生きた情<ココロ>の働きに、不具も欠陥もある筈がない。それ
> はそのまま分裂を知らず、観点を設けぬ、全的な認識
> 力である筈だ。(154)

Motoori firmly believes that, unaltered by acquired
knowledge or intellectual work, there is something fundamental in human experience, in which the human heart
reacts to things of this world. The way the human heart
moves is not as easy to fathom, as when one speaks of "my
heart" as injured or lost, since a human heart, always
complete and alive, moves as it reacts to things, directly and
intimately. It always provides an all-embracing perception,
which knows no division or no angle. (my translation)

Mono no aware, for Kobayashi, is a ceaseless action of the human heart. By urging readers to associate Faulknerian grief with
"aware(ness)" and ultimately with Kobayashi's *mono no aware*,
Oe seems to suggest that Faulknerian grief means something like
what Bergson called duration (Kobayashi is a Bergsonian), or the
sense of time—or time in motion—which the human heart feels
independently of the reason which tells us to grasp the world with
"division" and "angle."[2]
     As we will see later in this chapter, Oe metaphorically translates

Faulkner's conception of time, which is associated with grief, into such ideas or characters—that is, such metaphors—as *Kowasuhito* (the Destroyer), *mori no fushigi* (the wonder of the forest), *natsukashii toshi* (the year of nostalgia), "*ame no ki*" (the "rain tree"), and leap.[3] Oe's literary microcosm, based on his native village, is a spatial embodiment of what Faulkner calls "*is*." In other words, Oe's efforts to create his own Yoknapatawpha is an attempt to illustrate Faulkner's conception of time, which for Oe is best expressed in his favorite sentence in *If I Forget Thee, Jerusalem*: "*Between grief and nothing, I will take grief*" (273).

Here, however, we should not forget that Oe is a writer who is always politically motivated. In his apparently non-political association of grief with *aware* is also hidden a subversive intent. In this sense, Oe's challenge is also Quentin Compson's:

> And so as soon as I knew I couldn't see it, I began to wonder what time it was. Father said that constant speculation regarding the position of mechanical hands on an arbitrary dial which is a symptom of mind-function. Excrement Father said like sweating. And I saying All right. Wonder. Go on and wonder. (Faulkner, *The Sound and the Fury* 77)

Quentin's attitude toward time springs out of the sense of time both conveyed to him from his locality and inherited from his father and grandfather. It is rooted in his region, the South. Similarly, Oe's attempt to create his own Yoknapatawpha has a regional context. What Oe borrowed from Faulkner is not only the idea of a cosmos unified by the Bergsonian sense of time, but also the idea of a space marginalized by a regional sense of time different from the standard, central time. For Oe, Yoknapatawpha is a metaphor for such a space-time continuum that is paradoxically characterized by a sense of loss, or a sense of being deprived of time itself. Such a sense of loss or deprivation, however, creates a character like Quentin

Compson. Similarly, Oe finds in his own Yoknapatawpha a chance to subvert the authoritarian, central time of Japan and to seek the sense of time which is truly universal.

Curiously enough, Faulkner had already made a similar point when he wrote in his essay "To the Youth of Japan" that "out of your disaster and despair will come a group of Japanese writers whom all the world will want to listen to, who will speak not a Japanese truth but a universal truth" (83–84). Oe was twenty years old when the essay was first published in 1955. Forty years later, in his Nobel Prize acceptance speech, as if to respond to Faulkner's essay, Oe, speaking of his debt to Mikhail Bakhtin, said: "the image system [of grotesque realism or the culture of popular laughter] made it possible to seek literary methods of attaining the universal for someone like me, born and brought up in a peripheral, marginal, off-center region of a peripheral, marginal, off-center country" ("Japan, the Ambiguous, and Myself" 125). For Faulkner, the region means the South, or Mississippi, not America. For Oe, too, the region means his native village in Shikoku, not Japan. As Faulkner foretold in his essay, the universal truth for Oe should not be the Japanese truth. Although Charles Baker pointed out—though based on Faulkner's own remarks concerning Japan—the parallel relationship between Faulkner's post-bellum South and Japan after World War II in terms of common postcolonial position against "Northern imperialism" (1–4), for Oe, the equivalent of the American South is not Japan, but his own native village, which in *Dojidai gemu* and *M/T to mori no fushigi no monogatari* fought a fictional war against Japan's imperialism. This does not mean, however, that Oe exempts himself from Japanese cultural, or political, heritage. In the speech, Oe calls both Japan and himself the "ambiguous," suggesting the in-between positions of both Japan and himself, who are split between the Western and the Asiatic, the modern and the traditional (116–17). Oe's sense of ambiguity is reflected in his awareness of being a citizen of a country which is at once the victim and the perpetrator of the worldwide imperialism in the nineteenth and the twentieth centuries.

That ambiguity also rises in Oe as a writer whose works are an amalgam of both Western and Japanese literatures. In the Nobel Prize speech, Oe likens himself to W. B. Yeats, who was also split between the Irish and British heritages. Apart from whether or not he directly borrows from it, Oe here reminds us of a discussion on Yeats by his friend, Edward Said:

> For Yeats the overlapping he knew existed of his Irish nationalism with the English cultural heritage, which both dominated and empowered him, was bound to cause tension, and one may speculate that it was the pressure of this urgently political and secular tension that caused him to try to resolve it on a "higher," that is, nonpolitical level. The deeply eccentric and aestheticized histories he produced in *A Vision* and the later quasi-religious poems elevate the tension to an extra-worldly level, as if Ireland were best taken over, so to speak, at a level above that of the ground. (227)

We can see here the political origin of Yoknapatawpha, or the metaphorical use of one's native region. What is common to Yeats, Faulkner, and Oe, is their ambition to metaphorically elevate the regional into the universal or, to use a Faulknerian term, the apocryphal. Creating one's own Yoknapatawpha is an attempt to find in the regional the true universal which should be distinguished from the false universal represented by the central or standard time. For Oe, Yoknapatawpha is a means to object to the authoritarian Japan, especially to its authoritarian sense of time represented by the immortal presence of the Emperor. In the final section of the present chapter, after two sections which discuss the Faulknerian connection of Oe's metaphors—*Kowasuhito, mori no fushigi, natsukashii toshi,* "*ame no ki*," and leap—, we will look more closely at the political implications, or the subversive performances, of Oe's own Yoknapatawpha.

Faulkner's "*is*" and Oe's Metaphors

In the Jean Stein interview, Faulkner called Yoknapatawpha a "cosmos of my own" and himself "God" (Meriwether and Millgate 255). Although those words may bring up the image of a well-ordered universe, made especially to fit the author's own sense of order, that image would mislead us. On the contrary, Faulkner means that he tried to keep the universe in motion, or in constant change. Faulkner adds:

> The fact that I have moved my characters around in time successfully, at least in my own estimation, proves to me my own theory that time is a fluid condition which has no existence except in the momentary avatars of individual people. There is no such thing as *was*—only *is*. If *was* existed there would be no grief or sorrow. I like to think of the world I created as being a kind of keystone in the Universe; that, as small as that keystone is, if it were ever taken away, the universe itself would collapse. My last book will be the Doomsday Book, the Golden Book, of Yokna- patawpha County. Then I shall break the pencil and I'll have to stop. (Meriwether and Millgate 255)

Each individual is a "momentary avatar" of the time as a "fluid condition." Only within each individual does exist such a fluid time. If such a time within can be called life, another word for it is, "motion"; for Faulkner the "aim of every artist is to arrest motion, which is life" (253). For Faulkner, then, human life does not necessarily lead to death. Here is a Faulknerian paradox: "since man is mortal, the only immortality possible for him is to leave something behind him that is immortal since it will always move" (253). In mortality lies a chance for human immortality; each individual is an "avatar" of the fluid time. Conversely, if mortality is forgotten and immortality is sought for as such, time ceases to move. Faulkner rejects the idea of human immortality as such, as well as death itself—both represented as "was"—as a misconception of time. Instead, Faulkner insists that "is" is the true concept of time. "Is" signifies time through which mortality bears immortality, and in which life and death merge in one "fluid condition." "Grief" represents a continuing (e)motion of the human heart accompanying such a "fluid condition." For Faulkner, creating his own cosmos means to set up such a concept of time, that is, time as a "fluid condition," as the "keystone in the Universe."[4]

When Oe creates his own literary cosmos under the influence of Faulkner, he seems also to borrow from Faulkner his keystone, such a conception of time. The difference, if there is one, however, lies in the concreteness of Oe's "is"; Oe's "is" is embodied by a character, a thing, or an image, and apparently situated at the center of the narrative. For example, in *Dojidai gemu* (1979), Oe calls it *Kowasuhito* (the Destroyer).[5] The novel consists of six long letters written by the narrator-historian "I" to his sister who lives in their native village as a shrine maiden. In those letters, "I" attempts to construct the history of their village, based mostly on the stories "I" heard from his father and re-created in his own imagination. At the center of the history is *Kowasuhito*, the legendary creator of the village. *Kowasuhito* is ubiquitous. Every important figure in the history—even the village itself—embodies him. Simply put, *Kowasuhito* is Oe's metaphor for "is," or that which destroys "was."[6]

We have rather a clear evidence that Oe is indebted to Faulkner in characterizing *Kowasuhito* as a metaphor for "is." Oe probably refers to Old Ben, the bear, in *Go Down, Moses*. In the last letter of *Dojidai gemu*, "I" recalls his experience in childhood, in which he goes into the forest alone, and walks around, driven by a sense of duty, which was given to him in a dream, to "restore the whole of *Kowasuhito*" by tracing every part of his dead body, which, against the legend that the corpse of *Kowasuhito* was eaten by the villagers, is cut into pieces and buried all over the forest (*Dojidai gemu* 574). While walking, "I" feels the gaze of *Shirime*, a legendary killer of *Kowasuhito*. This reminds us of Old Ben, who, according to Sam, was watching Ike, who did not see him (Faulkner, *Go Down, Moses* 197). *Shirime* is *Kowasuhito*'s double. *Shirime* kills *Kowasuhito* under the latter's direction, as if they were in conspiracy. We can see the similar relationship in *Go Down, Moses*: Old Ben, the killed, chooses Boon and Lion, the killers, and then Sam instructs Boon in how to end his body. Old Ben is described as "furious immortality" (Faulkner, *Go Down, Moses* 186); similarly, *Kowasuhito* is called "man of immortality" 不死の人 (Oe, *Dojidai gemu* 193).

In *M/T to mori no fushigi no monogatari* (1986), a retelling of the same story as narrated in *Dojidai gemu*, yet with a change in gender— that is, from father to grandmother as "I"'s source, Oe stresses the role of the mysterious material in the forest called *mori no fushigi*, or the wonder of the forest, which has already appeared in *Dojidai gemu* as something extraterrestrial. *Mori no fushigi* is a variation, or a development, of the metaphor of *Kowasuhito*. At the end of the novel, *mori no fushigi* is explained as a place from which each of the villagers' souls—including the soul of *Kowasuhito*—is returned to this world after death. *Mori no fushigi* is called *omoto*, the source or the root (531). It is like the womb of the villagers' souls, and therefore, according to "I"'s grandmother, causes in the villagers a yearning or nostalgia for return throughout their lives (531–32).

In *Natsukashii toshi eno tegami* (1987), a fictional memoir written by the narrator-novelist, "I" (K-chan), for the memory of his spiritual guide, Brother Gii, we can see another metaphor for "*is.*" In the novel, Oe traces his own life and work, half fictionally and half actually, and turns it into a process of conversion, or a story of death and resurrection. Influenced by Dante, Yanagita Kunio (Japanese folklorist), and the Aborigine's idea of the eternal dream time, Brother Gii tries to build in their native village a "base," an ideal community, where each member can engage him/herself in the "matters of the soul." What is aimed at is to present a model of "this world, as well as the world beyond it" この世界の・またそれを超えた世界 (534, 535, 542, 566, 585). At the end of the novel, after the tragic death of Brother Gii, "I" decides to dedicate his remaining career as novelist to writing letters to *natsukashii toshi*—that is, the eternal year or recurring time in which "I"'s soul would meet Brother Gii's again and forever. *Natsukashii toshi* is a variation of Oe's metaphor for "*is*," the time as a "fluid condition."

Kowasuhito (the Destroyer) in *Dojidai gemu*, *mori no fushigi* (the wonder of the forest) in *M/T to mori no fushigi no monogatari*, and *natsukashii toshi* (the year of nostalgia) in *Natsukashii toshi eno tegami* are Oe's metaphors for "*is*." For Oe, as well as for Faulkner, such a metaphorical rendering of "*is*" makes the crux of the creation of Yoknapatawpha. Having "*is*" at its center, Yoknapatawpha itself becomes such a metaphor for "*is*."

Strictly speaking, however, Oe did not realize the metaphoricity of Yoknapatawpha until relatively later. At least, when he wrote *Dojidai gemu*, Oe had not yet understood his own Yoknapatawpha in terms of metaphors or metaphoricity. In *Shosetsu no hoho* (Methodology of the Novel, 1978), which was written at the same time as *Dojidai gemu* and published a year before the novel, Oe revealed, like a juggler who shows his hands, the methods used in the novel. There are two foci in *Shosetsu no hoho*: defamilialization of Russian Formalism and Mikhail Bakhtin's idea of grotesque realism, both of which Oe learned through Yamaguchi Masao's *Bunka to ryogisei* (Culture and Ambiguity, 1975). In the book, Oe mentions metaphor in two passages, but it is neither fully explicated nor even defined (*Shosetsu no hoho* 86, 99). Throughout the book, what should be later labeled metaphor is called *kotoba no shikake* (trick of words). This seems strange, because by the time he wrote the book, Oe must have learned about Jakobson's concepts of metaphor and metonymy through Yamaguchi, with whom he was personally acquainted. As far as *Bunka to ryogisei* is concerned, however, Jakobson is discussed mainly in the last chapter in terms of the opposition between poetic and daily languages, not between metaphor and metonymy (276–88).

We have to wait for *"Ame no ki" o kiku onnatachi* (Women Who Listen to the "Rain Tree," 1982) to see Oe discuss metaphor intensively. The novel, in this sense, is a key to understanding Oe's metaphorical use of Yoknapatawpha. Although the novel is not part of Oe's saga concerning Yoknapatawpha-like creation, we can see here another instance in which Oe metaphorically translates Faulkner's "*is*" into an image or idea. In the Jean Stein interview, Faulkner calls the (e)motion which accompanies "*is*" "grief." "Grief," in this sense, is not so much a feeling as an idea which supports Faulkner's conception of time. "'Ame no ki' o kiku onnatachi," the title piece of the collection of short stories *"Ame no ki" o kiku onnatachi*, is concerned with such an idea of grief.

Grief is one of the words which Oe most frequently mentions both in his novels and essays. In some cases, Oe even refers to, as its source, not only *If I Forget Thee, Jerusalem* but also Faulkner's letters and biographies. For example, discussing the word "grief" which appears in Faulkner's letter to Joan Williams,[7] Oe writes:

フォークナーという大作家の内部に、悲嘆^{グリーフ}という言葉が、このような文脈のなかで生きる要素として懐胎され、小説に表現され、それからも二十年にわたって、かれの人間としてのありように影響しつづける——この言葉によってのみ表現されうる、内的なある局面をかれが持つということは、すでにフォークナーの肉体と精神の一部分をこの言葉がつくっている、ということですらあるでしょう——その様子を、僕は曲りなりにも伝達しえたのではないでしょうか? (*Shosetsu no takurami, chi no tanoshimi* 52)

Within Faulkner, the great writer, the word grief is conceived in a context like this [that is, the affair] as an element that lives, represented in his novel, and, over the following twenty years, still keeps affecting the way he is—since he has an aspect within himself that can be expressed by no other word than that, it might be the case that that word had already made part of Faulkner's body and spirit—

[In *"Ame no ki" o kiku onnatachi*] didn't I somehow suc-
ceed in representing all this? (my translation)

Oe suggests that the word, or the idea of, grief meant so much to
Faulkner for such a long period of time, that it became a part of
Faulkner himself, or even that it had always been Faulkner himself.
Grief, in this sense, becomes a metaphor for the Faulkner within,
which is hidden from Faulkner the "great writer." Oe says that *"Ame
no ki" o kiku onnatachi* was written to convey such a metaphorical
function that the word grief has. Here grief is a metaphor for the way
Faulkner lives in "*is*," that is, the time as a "fluid condition." In this
sense, grief expresses a sense of temporal order hidden from Faulkner's life as "great writer," which pretends to make up his whole life.
In *"Ame no ki" o kiku onnatachi*, especially in "'Ame no ki' o kiku
onnatachi," Oe depicts the way grief comes up in Faulkner's, and
more generally, a modern person's, psyche from where it is hidden, or
repressed. In "'Ame no ki' o kiku onnatachi," the "rain tree" and grief
collaterally function as metaphors for such a repressed sense of time.

 "Ame no ki" o kiku onnatachi is a collection of five short stories,
which, in the manner of Faulkner's *Go Down, Moses*, are related to
each other. Like Oe's other novels or collections of short stories, such
as *Warera no kyouki o ikinobiru michi o oshieyo* (Teach Us to
Outgrow Our Madness, 1969), *Atarashii hitoyo mezameyo* (trans. as
Rouse Up O Young Men of the New Age! 1983), and *Kaba ni
kamareru* (Bitten by a Hippo, 1985), five short stories in *"Ame no ki"
o kiku onnatachi*—that is, "Atama no ii 'ame no ki'" (The Ingenious
"Rain Tree"),[8] "'Ame no ki' o kiku onnatachi" (Women Who Listen
to the "Rain Tree"), "'Ame no ki' no kubitsuriotoko" (Man Hanging
Himself from the "Rain Tree"), "Sakasama ni tatsu 'ame no ki'" (The
"Rain Tree" Standing Upside Down), and "Oyogu otoko: mizu no
nakano 'ame no ki'" (The Swimming Man: the "Rain Tree" in the
Water)—are narrated by the character-narrator "I," who is Oe's
persona, even if somewhat caricatured. As a whole, the book depicts
the process in which the novelist "I" comes to conceive the "rain tree"

as a metaphor for the cosmos in which he lives. At the same time, however, "I" realizes that the "rain tree" appears only through its introverted, distorted, and displaced images: as the titles indicate, the "rain tree" is "ingenious"; it is associated with the image of "women who listen to" it; it is also associated with a "man hanging himself from" it; it is "standing upside down"; it lies "in the water." It should be noted here that we are watching a Freudian scene: the "rain tree" is the metaphor for the repressed, and it returns to "I" despite/because of repression.

As Enomoto Masaki points out, Oe's "rain tree" might also be representing the Cosmic Tree, which Oe learned through reading Mircea Eliade (34–36). According to Eliade, the Cosmic Tree, "whose roots plunged down into Hell, and whose branches reached to Heaven" (44), is related to the symbolism of the center of the universe (Axis Mundi), through which "communication with Heaven and Hell may be realized," and "by transcending the Universe, the created world, one also transcends time and achieves *stasis*—the eternal non-temporal present" (75). The Cosmic Tree is a metaphor for the center of the universe; Oe's "rain tree" then is a metaphor for the Cosmic Tree, and ultimately for the center of the universe. Moreover, the center of the universe can also be regarded as a metaphor for a fundamental sense of order, which should connect every triune world—that is, heaven, this surface world, and hell—to the two ultimate realms of life and death. In this sense, Oe's "rain tree" is another expression of what Faulkner calls "*is*," that is, the conception of time as a "fluid condition" which paradoxically connects mortality and immortality.

However, there is one thing that we should not dismiss: what *"Ame no ki" o kiku onnatachi* is concerned with is not how we hold this common sense of order, but how we are alienated from it. For Oe, the metaphor of the "rain tree" is a way to glimpse such an order, no matter how introverted, distorted, and displaced—or repressed—it may be in our psyche. For Freud, repression is basically a defense mechanism. For Oe, too, repression is part of the mechanism in which we defend our daily, normal lives from the fundamental order, which might suddenly erupt in our minds and cause a mental disorder, a wish for escape from modern life, and a wish to go home, to the womb, or to death.

In "Atama no ii 'ame no ki,'" the first short story of *"Ame no ki" o kiku onnatachi*, "I" is invited to a seminar held in Hawaii, and, during a party held at a madhouse, taken out by the superintendent of the house to see what is called by the local inhabitants the "rain tree." The superintendent describes the tree as "ingenious" because it can keep on its leaves the water gotten from the shower of the previous night and water itself the next day. "I" cannot see the tree because it is already dark; instead, he only sees "the darkness where the tree should be" 樹木がそこにあるはずの暗闇 (14). At the end of the story, nurses and guards are found tied up and the party turns out being held by the patients. It is easy to see here the borrowing of the plot of Edgar Allan Poe's "The System of Doctor Tarr and Professor Fether," in which the narrator gets to know the truth about the "soothing system." In Oe's short story, the party held by lunatics serves as a chance for "I" to get to know the "rain tree." The party held by lunatics represents the world in a mess. However, it is only in the world in a mess that "I" can feel the presence of the "rain tree" in the dark of the night. Here the "rain tree" already serves as metaphor for something repressed in a modern person's psyche.

In "Atama no ii 'ame no ki,'" however, Oe has not yet understood the "rain tree" as metaphor. As Enomoto points out, in "Atama no ii 'ame no ki,'" Oe never mentions it as metaphor (34). It is through writing the second short story, "'Ame no ki' o kiku onnatachi," which was published in November 1981, that Oe begins to recognize the function of the "rain tree" in "Atama no ii 'ame no ki" as metaphor. In this sense, "'Ame no ki' o kiku onnatachi" is not so much a sequel to "Atama no ii 'ame no ki'" as a text which describes how the previous short story about the "rain tree" was written. (To maintain the fictionality, Oe never allows "I" in "'Ame no ki' o kiku onnatachi" to refer to the previous short story as "Atama no ii 'ame no ki.'") "'Ame

no ki' o kiku onnatachi" is a meta-narrative concerning the making of
"Atama no ii 'ame no ki.'"

At the beginning of "'Ame no ki' o kiku onnatachi," "I" goes to
the premiere of his friend T's piece for two marimbas and vibraphone,
which T has composed based on the theme taken from "I"'s short
story on the "rain tree."[9] Listening to the music, "I" realizes that his
short story was aimed at "presenting the metaphor of the "rain tree"
as hanging over the sky"; 「雨の木」の暗喩をひとつ宙に架けるよう
にして提示すること (37). "I" feels that T's music is teaching him
what has been repressed in his own short story:

> そして僕がこの小説で表現したかったものは、その
> 「雨の木」の確かな幻であって、それはほかならぬ僕
> にとっての、この宇宙の暗喩だと感じたのである。自
> 分がそのなかにかこみこまれて存在しているありかた、
> そのありかた自体によって把握している、この宇宙。
> それがいまモデルとして「雨の木」のかたちをとり、
> 宙空にかかっているのだと。(39)

> What I wanted to express in the short story is a clear vision
> of the "rain tree," which, for none else but me, was a meta-
> phor for this universe. This universe—including the way I
> exist enclosed in it, and that which I grasp through the way
> it is—is hanging over the sky in the form of the "rain tree"
> as model. (my translation)

However, T's music, played by two male and one female players, also
urges him to remember another element, that is, a memory of a
triangular love relationship that has been repressed in his psyche:

> そのうち音楽はヴィブラフォンと二台のマリンバによ
> る、およそ闊達な、大きい骨格とひろびろした展望の
> 世界に移行した。僕はひとり魂を浄化されたように、
> なお「雨の木」の宇宙モデルの影響下にあって、息を

とめ、涙を流していたのである。そしてその涙には、
僕がハワイでのセミナー期間に経験しながら、あの短
編に書くことのなかった出来事が、直接に関係してい
るとも自覚された。・・・僕がハワイで経験しながら、
むしろそれを隠蔽するためのように、それぬきの話と
して「雨の木」の話を書いていた間、僕はある悲嘆の
気分につきまとわれていたのであった。(39)

In the meantime, the music has transferred to the world
with quite a generous, widely framed, and spacious perspective. I was shedding tears, breathless, still under the
influence of the model of the universe represented by the
"rain tree," as if my soul had been alone purified. And I was
aware that my tears had something to do with the incident I
had experienced in Hawaii, yet had not written in the short
story. . . . While I was writing the story about the "rain
tree," without mentioning the incident in Hawaii, even as if
I would rather try to suppress it, the feeling of grief haunted
me. (my translation)

At a seminar held in Hawaii, "I" is approached by his old friend,
Takayasu Katchan, with a proposal that they co-author a novel in
which "men and women live in various places on this earth each in his
or her own way, yet are all chosen to take on the task of fighting
against the fate of modern world, and set to work in response to an
eagle beating its wings at the periphery of the universe" (my
translation); 地球上の様ざまな場所に、それぞれ別べつに生きる男女
たち、しかもそろって現代世界の運命打開に責任のある秀れた男女た
ちが、宇宙のへりでの鷲の羽ばたきに感応して行動をおこす (58). But
"I" has already known that the idea of the novel originally belongs to
Saiki, their common friend, who died of leukemia. "I" just listens to
Takayasu, trying to refuse his proposal implicitly. At night, Takayasu
visits "I" with a woman, called Penny, whom he introduces as a call
girl, and offers her to "I." "I" refuses them again. About half a year

later, "I" receives a letter from Penny and is asked once again to consider co-authoring the novel with Takayasu. Instead of co-authoring the novel about the "eagle," "I" publishes a short story about the "rain tree" on his own. About three months later, "I" receives another letter from Penny, who turns out to be Takayasu's wife, and knows that Takayasu, after days of disappointment, died in an accident.

Here, we come across borrowings from Faulkner's two novels: *If I Forget Thee, Jerusalem* and *The Town*. "I" calls his feeling concerning Takayasu and Penny "grief" in English. "Grief" is a word that Takayasu often used when he was an undergraduate majoring in English literature. As an undergraduate, Takayasu went to America to attend Faulkner's lectures at the University of Virginia. In a letter from America, Takayasu wrote to "I" that in a seminar Faulkner had answered a student by saying that "between grief and nothing, man will take grief always" (42).[10] His former classmates doubted Takayasu's report, because they all knew that the phrase was the most famous part in *If I Forget Thee, Jerusalem* (then, *The Wild Palms*). Later, *Faulkner in the University* was published, and "I" found out that Takayasu was right. Since then, the word "grief" became a key word allowing "I" to remember Takayasu.

Moreover, we can see a borrowing from *The Town* in the triangular relationship into which Takayasu tried to involve "I" with Penny, his wife. It is not so much Takayasu as Penny herself who willed to offer herself to "I" in order to help her husband. Obviously, this triangular relationship is based on the relationship between Gavin, Eula and Flem in *The Town*. We can attest to this borrowing through the fact that, in July 1981, exactly when Oe was writing "'Ame no ki' o kiku onnatachi," Oe gave a speech on Faulkner, and discussed the Snopes trilogy, *If I Forget Thee, Jerusalem* and *Absalom, Absalom!* (I will discuss the speech extensively in the following chapter on the feminine, since the speech is concerned with not so much grief and time as the relationship between male and female characters in Faulkner.)

These borrowings from Faulkner are not gratuitous, since, as seen above, "'Ame no ki' o kiku onnatachi" is concerned with Faulkner's own affair with Joan Williams, or, more precisely, with the idea of grief which is associated with the affair. Here, as we have seen at the beginning of this chapter, Oe puns on the word "grief." In the short story, Penny uses the Japanese word "AWARE," as the translation of the English word "grief," to express her grief for Takayasu, her husband. However, in view of the influence of *The Town*, we should add another pun here. Conversely, the Japanese word *aware* can be translated into English as compassion or pity. "Compassion" and "pity" are the words with which, in *The Town*, Gavin describes Eula's attitude toward him, when she comes to offer herself to him (94). Of course, Gavin is wrong, because there is more in Eula than just compassion and pity. Here, we can see Oe's own interpretation of Eula's motives. By making Penny express "AWARE" to her husband, Oe suggests that he sees the same "AWARE," not compassion and pity, in Eula's attitude toward Gavin, and also Williams' attitude toward Faulkner. In this sense, the relationship between Faulkner and Williams and that of Gavin and Eula are the models of that between Penny and Takayasu, and even that between Penny and "I," to whom Penny offers herself.

At the end of "'Ame no ki' o kiku onnatachi," "I" recalls the second letter from Penny, in which she calls the "rain tree" in his short story a "metaphor," and at the same time says that she believes in the existence of the "rain tree." It is not T's music but this second letter from Penny that makes "I" realize for the first time that the "rain tree" is a metaphor. Curiously, however, the fact is repressed in "I"'s psyche until he listens to T's music. Penny believes that the "rain tree" is actual, because she knows that "I" met Takayasu at the madhouse. Takayasu was a patient there. Penny intuitively knows that "I"'s short story has repressed the meeting. Penny writes: "I also read your short story. Although I did not tell Takayasu, I do not think that the tree is a mere metaphor. I think that there is the "rain tree" in actuality. In the short story, you write that you did not see the tree, but

I think that you must have seen it" (my translation); 私もあの小説を
読んだ。高安には黙っていたが、私はあの樹木が、単なる暗喩だとは
思わない。現実に「雨の木」はあると思う。また小説では、あなたが
「雨の木」を見なかったと書いてあったが、私はあなたが見たはずだ
と思う (78). Penny is a guide who leads "I" into his own psyche to
see what is repressed. We can see here the function of Oe's metaphor:
she says that "I" must have seen the tree, but he does not think so;
later, listening to T's music, that is, led by T as his guide, he sees it
once again, but it is lost again; "I," or Oe, writes more short stories
concerning the "rain tree," but the tree itself does not appear; the
guides always say that it was there and "I" actually saw it, but "I"
does not think so.

The "rain tree" is a metaphor for the sense of time repressed in
"I"'s psyche. By expressing "AWARE," that is, grief, to her husband,
Penny also reminds "I," who keeps saying that "we get old to die" 人
が死にむけて年をとる (34), that he is another Takayasu, who has lost
the sense of time in which life lies in death, and also oblivion and
memory, which Penny mentions in the same letter referring to
Malcolm Lowry (78–79), are in one "fluid condition." Not that Penny
knows the metaphorical connection between the "rain tree" and
"AWARE." She simply says that she believes in the actuality of the
"rain tree" and, at the same time, feels "AWARE" for her dead
husband. For "I," and also for us readers, however, they together
appear as metaphors for the same sense of order, or the concept of
time, which Faulkner called "is."

Leap to Life: *The Sound and the Fury, Absalom, Absalom!* and *The Silent Cry*

As we have seen above, in *Dojidai gemu, Mori no fushigi no
monogatari, Natsukashii toshi e no tegami,* Oe turns Faulkner's "is"
into such metaphors as *Kowasuhito, mori no fushigi, natsukashii toshi.*
Also, as we have seen with "'*Ame no ki*' o kiku onnatachi," Oe
provided the metaphor of the "*ame no ki*," or the "rain tree," with the

function of looking into the repressed in "I"'s psyche. We can see that Oe's attempts are consistently aimed at giving the reader the image of time which exists in the heart of each individual, that is, time as duration. Now we turn to *Man'en gannen no futtoboru*, or *The Silent Cry*, the first novel in which Oe intentionally created his own Yoknapatawpha-like microcosm. In this novel, as Faulkner placed a sense of time, represented by the metaphor of *"is,"* at the center of his creation, Oe provides his own cosmos with a sense of time that is metaphorically represented by an idea of leap. Although, at this point, Oe has not yet developed a theory of metaphor, we can see in the idea of leap a predecessor to the metaphors that Oe intentionally uses in his later novels. In *The Silent Cry* the idea of leap is represented by characters' decisions to make a change in their lives. Making a change in one's life means to restore the *"is"* of each individual.

It is well known that Oe read Faulkner when he was preparing to write *The Silent Cry*. We can see rather an apparent parallel between *The Silent Cry* and, in particular, *Absalom, Absalom!* For Oe, *Absalom, Absalom!* provides not only a model of Yoknapatawpha-like literary microcosm but also a way to express *"is."* There are, of course, differences in the treatment of *"is"* between *Absalom, Absalom!* and *The Silent Cry*. To clarify the points of comparison between *Absalom, Absalom!* and *The Silent Cry*, I will draw on the psychoanalytic readings of *Absalom, Absalom!* as presented by John T. Irwin and Doreen Fowler. Conspicuously, the psychoanalytic readings of *Absalom, Absalom!* have made it easier to believe that *Absalom, Absalom!* provides readers with a clue to understanding Quentin's suicide in *The Sound and the Fury*; in fact, *Absalom, Absalom!* can even seem to repeat the Quentin section in *The Sound and the Fury*. At the point of writing *The Silent Cry*, Oe could never have read Irwin or Fowler. Nevertheless, it seems that the crux of *The Silent Cry* has been conceived in opposition to the view of death presented in psychoanalytic readings of *The Sound and the Fury* and *Absalom, Absalom!* What is at issue is a somewhat stale question: why did Quentin kill himself?

In *The Silent Cry*, the central issue on which Mitsu and Takashi quarrel is how their great-grandfather's younger brother died. Mitsu and Taka contradict each other almost to the end of the novel. In the beginning, Taka insists that the great-grandfather's younger brother was brave enough to stick to the 1860 riot, which he had caused, and get killed by the great-grandfather who opposed his brother. On the other hand, Mitsu denies his great-grandfather's brother's braveness and insists that, with the help of the great-grandfather, he fled after the riot and lived and died happily in Tokyo. Taka tries to prove his theory of the heroic life and death of his great-grandfather's younger brother by imitating him and himself leading the looting of the supermarket owned by a Korean called the "Emperor of the supermarkets." Mitsu, however, becomes more convinced of his own theory after talking to the chief priest of the temple. The priest assumes that the death of Brother S (the second of the Nedokoro brothers, while Mitsu is the third, and Taka the fourth), who sacrificed himself in 1945 in compensation for the attack on the Koreans by the youths of the village, can be also regarded as an act of compensation for his great-grandfather's younger brother's flight from the village eighty-four years before. In the meantime, with musical effects from the traditional *nenbutsu-odori*, Taka tries to keep awake in the villagers' minds a connection between the present event and the 1860 riot. On the other hand, Mitsu finds in the letters of the great-grandfather's brother, which the chief priest of the temple discovered, the evidence of his flight and life after the riot. At the novel's climax, Taka wishes to be lynched by the villages for the death of a village girl, whom he insists he has tried to rape and then killed, and also confesses that he is responsible for the suicide of their mentally retarded sister, with whom he committed incest. However, Mitsu still suspects that what Taka really wants is not such a brave and heroic self-punishment, but rather, as the great-grandfather's brother did, a dissuasion by his older brother and a guarantee of the life hereafter. After the confession, Taka commits suicide by shooting himself, while Mitsu suffers from a sense of repetition, which comes as a false memory in which he has seen a lot of dead people, who look like Taka, in this same place before.

It is not difficult to point out that this relationship between Mitsu and Taka resembles that of Quentin and Shreve in Faulkner's *Absalom, Absalom!*[11] Just as the past is re-created in the present through the imaginative collaboration between Quentin and Shreve, so what happened to great-grandfather's brother a hundred years before is revealed only through the psychological conflict between Mitsu and Taka. It is not until the final chapter, however, that Mitsu comes to know the truth about the great-grandfather's brother. He then realizes that, apart from the details, Taka was right. A cellar is discovered along with many books and documents at the site of the destroyed storehouse. Mitsu realizes for the first time that the great-grandfather's brother confined himself to the cellar as a form of self-punishment. Moreover, Mitsu finds out that after successfully leading another riot without bloodshed in 1871, the great-grand-father's brother confined himself to the cellar for the rest of his life, simply reading books and other documents brought in by the great-grandfather and writing letters in which he pretended to live far from home.

In the final chapter of *Absalom, Absalom!* Quentin comes to know the meaning of the story of Henry and Bon, which has been re-created through the collaboration with Shreve. Quentin recalls the scene in which he meets Henry, who has been confining himself in the Sutpen mansion, waiting for death. It seems rather obvious that Oe borrowed this figure of Henry, who comes home forty-five years after killing Bon and lives four more years in self-confinement, thinking of death. Quentin meets Henry on the night of the day in the summer of 1909, that is, the day when he met Rosa. It is, however, on the January night of 1910 in his room at Harvard, after he re-created the past incident through collaboration with Shreve, that Quentin realizes the mean-ing of the meeting with Henry for the first time. Through the collaboration, Quentin comes to see in Henry his double and is afflicted by the sense of facing something hidden, or repressed, deep in his psyche. It is only with this sense of the so-called return of the repressed that Quentin can recall the meeting with Henry as something crucial for himself, that is, as something which makes him think "Nevermore of peace" (298). In this sense, it is not when Quentin actually met Henry but when he recalled the meeting that Quentin's psychological struggle with the Sutpen story reaches its real turning point. In a similar manner, in *The Silent Cry*, the turning point in Mitsu's reluctant pursuit of the truth about the great-grandfather's brother is brought to light by the discovery of the cellar in which the great-grandfather's brother confined himself to his death. It is only with this imaginary meeting with the great-grandfather's brother that Mitsu faces the past with sincerity.

The scene of Quentin's encounter with Henry is narrated as a double recollection: Quentin recalls in his room at Harvard the scene in which he recalled meeting Henry after sending Rosa to her house and coming back to his own. The scene of meeting Henry has been hidden, or repressed, thus dually in Quentin's psyche until the collaboration with Shreve forces, or allows, him to return to it:

> 'I ought to bathe,' he thought: then he was lying on the bed, naked, swabbing his body steadily with the discarded shirt, sweating still, panting: so that when, his eye-muscles aching and straining into the darkness and the almost dried shirt still clutched in his hand, he said 'I have been asleep' it was all the same, there was no difference: walking or sleeping he walked down that upper hall between the scaling walls and beneath the cracked ceiling, toward the faint light which fell outward from the last door and paused there, saying 'No. No' and then 'Only I must. I have to' and went in, entered the bare stale room whose shutters were closed too. (Faulkner, *Absalom, Absalom!* 298)

In order to reach the scene of meeting Henry, Quentin must first go through the scene of lying on the bed in his, or his father's, house.

The switch of scenes takes place between the phrases "there was no difference" and "waking or sleeping," but the contents of both phrases suggest the denial of the switch itself. It is as if the first scene in the father's house were trying vainly to force a difference between the present Quentin who is recalling and the Quentin, or Henry, who is recalled. In other words, it is as if the first scene were trying to repress, in vain, the return of the scene of meeting Henry in Quentin's psyche. What we see here fits precisely what John T. Irwin describes as the mechanism of the return of the repressed:

> we can see the necessary link between the repetition compulsion and repression. Freud points out that whatever is repressed will inevitably return. It is as if the act of repression endowed the repressed material with the repetition compulsion. But the repressed can return only through a displacement; only by being different can it slip past the conscious defenses to reveal itself as the same. But once it reveals itself as the same, the ego under the influence of the superego attempts to re-press it. Thus, in the very mechanism of repression, the return of the repressed, re-repression, and re-return, we find an explanation for what Freud, quoting Nietzsche, called in *Beyond the Pleasure Principle* "this 'perpetual recurrence of the same thing'"—the way in which the repressed by continually being different continually reconstitutes itself as the same. (94)

In Freud's *Beyond the Pleasure Principle*, the "perpetual recurrence of the same thing" is mentioned to explain the phenomenon in which a person's character, or fate, is expressed in the repetition of his or her same experiences. What interests Freud most, however, is the phenomenon in which a person passively comes across the same experiences again and again: for example, Freud refers to a woman who was predeceased by three husbands (24). It is in such a passive repetition, not the active repetition in which the repetition is apparently caused by the person's own actions, that Freud suspects an instinct, which overrides the pleasure principle. The hypothesis of the death instinct is based on the observation of such phenomena, which Freud elsewhere calls uncanny. Quentin passively meets Henry. If it were not for Rosa, Quentin could not have a chance to meet Henry. In like manner, Quentin passively collaborates with Shreve on the Sutpen story. At Harvard, Quentin happens to meet Shreve as a collaborator. We can assume that if it were not for Shreve, Quentin could have avoided re-creating the scene of meeting Henry.

Henry is repressed in Quentin's psyche. Henry is Quentin's double, in the sense that he is someone whose presence makes Quentin feel uncanny. Irwin argues that Bon is also Quentin's double, and that Henry represents Quentin's bright double—the "ego controlled by the superego"—and Bon his dark double—the "ego shadowed by the unconscious" (37). Henry kills Bon, that is, punishes his own desire. To meet Henry means for Quentin to meet his own fate, that is, the necessity of punishing himself—that is, killing himself. Not only Henry but also this whole relationship, or fate, is repressed in Quentin's psyche.

From the beginning, *The Silent Cry* also revolves around an uncanny repetition of three pairs of older and younger brothers: the great-grandfather and his younger brother; the oldest brother and Brother S; and Mitsu and Taka. The great-grandfather's younger brother is Taka's double, but he is also Mitsu's double, because Taka is Mitsu's double. Moreover, if we follow Irwin's use of the idea of bright and dark doubles, the great-grandfather is Mitsu's bright double, and the great-grandfather's younger brother his dark double. In this sense, the discovery of the cellar in which the great-grandfather's brother confined himself should mean for Mitsu the return of the repressed. In *Absalom, Absalom!* Quentin recalls the scene of meeting Henry through double recollection. Similarly, in *The Silent Cry*, the truth about the great-grandfather's brother is revealed to Mitsu through a double process.

The discovery that the great-grandfather did not kill his brother, but helped him to live under self-confinement, or even took care of him until his death, leads Mitsu to his decision to accept the secure job of English teacher—that is, to keep living like his great-grandfather, who "lived out their lives in vague appreciation, unwilling to allow the urgent inner demand for sudden, unscheduled leaps forward to grow to the point where action was necessary" (271); 不連続な飛躍を強いるあるものを自分の内側に発育させてそれと対決することを望まず、漠然と不安に生き延びる(444).[12] At this point, Mitsu's mind—particularly, Mitsu's "ego controlled by superego"—is still trying to repress the true implication of the discovery of the cellar. It is his wife, Natsumiko, who hints what has been truly repressed in Mitsu's psyche and persuades him to take the job of interpreter in Africa:

> あなたは鷹に対抗するために、自分のなかの鷹的なものを故意に排除して生きてきたのでしょう?蜜、もう鷹は死んだのだから、あなたも自分自身に対して公平にならなければならないわ。あなたの曾祖父さんの弟と鷹をむすぶものが、鷹のつくりあげた幻影ではなかったと蜜が了解した以上は、蜜自身も自分のなかに、かれらと共有するものを確かめてみるべきでしょう?それに蜜が、死んでしまった鷹を正当に記憶し続けようとしているのなら、なおさらそうしなければならない筈でしょう?(446)

> I think the need to oppose Taka has always made you deliberately reject the things that resembled him in you. But Taka's dead, Mitsu, so you should be fairer to yourself. Now you've seen that the ties between your great-grandfather's brother and Taka weren't just an illusion created by Taka, why don't you try to find out what you share with them yourself? It's even more important to do so now, isn't it, if you want to keep your memory of Taka straight? (272)

Natsumiko suggests that Mitsu should try to remember Taka correctly, that is, to play the role of his great-grandfather, who turned out to be not the oppressor of his younger brother but rather his ally. And at the same time, she urges him also to face the Taka—that is, the repressed—in himself. Natsumiko suggests, in short, that Mitsu should realize how he has forced on himself a distorted view concerning the relationship between his own "ego controlled by superego" and "ego shadowed by the unconscious." What is stressed in *Absalom, Absalom!*, if we follow Irwin, is Quentin's struggle with what is repressed in his psyche; hence comes his reluctant identification with Henry. In *The Silent Cry*, Mitsu is also reluctant to know about what has been repressed in his psyche. Quentin's fate is to repeat Henry, who has returned home to die. Mitsu's own interpretation of his fate is revised by his wife and re-presented as a new life in Africa, a place far from home.

Both *Absalom, Absalom!* and *The Silent Cry* are thus concerned with repetition. In his novel, however, Oe seems deliberately to characterize Mitsu's repetition of his doubles as something different from Quentin's. For Quentin, repetition ultimately comes to mean returning home, to the womb, and to the stage before life—that is, death. Doreen Fowler makes the point:

> Like life, which, according to Freud, doubles back upon itself, seeking to "return to lifelessness," a palindrome objectifies a desire to retrieve what was before; in this case, the repetitive form is an analogue for Henry's return home and for his dissolution into the environment. Along with these other signs, it is a formulation of the repressed. The meaning, then, that has so long eluded us is at last before us. What is repressed in the unconscious? Inside the dark house, Quentin, Shreve, and Miss Rosa find the desire to return to the origin, to restore a former inertia; they find a death wish. (*Faulkner* 124)

Quentin's repetition is directed backward, as Sartre once pointed out in his essay on *The Sound and the Fury*. In *Absalom, Absalom!* Quentin looks back at Henry, his predecessor, and says, "I am older at twenty than a lot of people who have died" (301). Quentin feels that he is standing at the end of the line, looking only backward, only at the people who have died. Henry, his predecessor, was also at the end of the line, looking only backward, dying without leaving his own children, but himself returning to childhood or even to the womb. In Freudian reading, this backward repetition is called regression:

> The result of Henry's murder of his black half brother is the kind of regression that one would expect from the suicidal murder of the double: Henry ends his life hidden in the womb of the family home where, helpless as a child, he is nursed by his black half sister Clytie. In a way, Henry's end repeats the fate of his maternal grandfather who at the beginning of the Civil War nailed himself into the attic of his home and who, though cared for by his daughter Rosa, eventually starved himself to death. (Irwin 50)

Henry's regression is also Quentin's. When Quentin meets Henry, he has already been involved in Henry's regression:

> And you are ——?
> Henry Sutpen.
> And you have been here ——?
> Four years.
> And you came home ——?
> To die. Yes.
> To die?
> Yes. To die.
> And you have been here ——?
> Four years.
> And you are ——?

Henry Sutpen. (Faulkner, *Absalom, Absalom!* 298)

Quentin does not ask Henry, "who are you?" "how long have you been here?" or "why are you here?" Instead, he asks, "and you are?" "and you have been here?" or "and you came home?" as if he has already known the answers. Or, in other words, it seems as if Henry were simply repeating what Quentin had said to himself in his mind. The scene suggests that everything has already happened in Quentin's psyche. In Quentin's unconscious, at least, it has been already and always self-evident that his double, or he himself, should come home to die.[13]

Repetition in *The Silent Cry*, on the other hand, does not entail regression toward death. In a somewhat far-fetched way, Oe has his character-narrator Mitsu depart for a new world, even if it would not be completely new as long as it is a result of Mitsu's consultation with his doubles. In order to break away from the regressive repetition seen in *Absalom, Absalom!*, Oe forces Mitsu to move forward—that is, to seek life—in two contradicting occasions: to leave home and to restore a home. As Natsumiko suggests, Mitsu decides to go to Africa as an interpreter, and also to accept two children—that is, the mentally handicapped son whom they have left in an institution and a child which Natsumiko has conceived by Taka.

For Mitsu, to leave home for Africa means to return home to Africa. Africa is Mitsu's home in the sense that the Taka in himself is his home. Unlike Henry's or Quentin's home, however, home for Mitsu is not death. Taka wished death and killed himself, believing that his great-grandfather's brother, his predecessor, had wished self-punishment and been killed in a riot by his older brother. Mitsu knows that Taka was wrong. Nevertheless, Mitsu thinks that Taka has the advantage, since Taka was right in the sense that he told his own truth. Mitsu comes to realize that Taka came home in his psyche by killing himself: "[I]n that final moment when he stood facing the muzzle that was to split the naked upper half of his body into in a mass of ripe pomegranates, he'd succeeded in achieving self-integration, in securing for himself an identity given consistency by his desire to be like great-grandfather's brother" (270); 鷹四は、最後にかれの裸の上半身を柘榴のようにする銃孔に向って立った瞬間に、曾祖父の弟にならうべき熱望につらぬかれた自分の identity を確認し、自己統一をとげた (442). What is stressed here is that there was such a moment when Taka finally decided to kill himself. Like Henry, Taka comes home to die. But it is only at that last moment when he finally decides to kill himself. This moment seems to be the point where *The Silent Cry* finally converges. If we can say that home in *Absalom, Absalom!* is death, we should say that home in *The Silent Cry* is a moment before death.

Here, we have to ask, after so much argument on doubling in *Absalom, Absalom!*, if it is really true that Quentin's suicide has something to do with his meeting with Henry. In the re-created scene, Henry tells Quentin that he has come home to die. But Henry also says that he has been in the mansion for four years, suggesting that he has not been able to kill himself for four years. In the end, Henry dies in fire, but we are not sure whether Henry killed himself. Even if he might have wanted to kill himself for a long time, it might also be the case that Henry asked Clytie to make the final decision. In *The Sound and the Fury*, Quentin kills himself. But it is not certain when he decided to kill himself, or what finally made him decide. Indeed, psychoanalysis filled the gap between *Absalom, Absalom!* and *The Sound and the Fury*, but it does not explain the gap between the Henry who is waiting for death and the Henry who actually died, or the possible gap between the Quentin depicted in both novels and the Quentin who actually killed himself. There is always a gap, or a void, between the one who is thinking of death and the one who actually killed him/herself. A death wish is supposed to inhere in every living being, not just to Henry or Quentin alone. Even supposing it is true that a living being instinctively wishes death, it still does not follow that Henry and Quentin killed themselves because of a death wish. What psychoanalysis points out as the death wish does not explain how Henry died or why Quentin killed himself.

The challenge of *The Silent Cry* is to look into such a void, which emerges a moment before one kills him/herself. In other words, it is to bring into the reading of *The Sound and the Fury* and *Absalom, Absalom!* the idea of a leap, or a last-second decision. Mitsu realizes that Taka, who, like Quentin and Henry, had wanted to die for a long time, finally got the energy by telling the "truth":

> 「本当の事」がおれに見きわめられていない以上、すなわちおれは死に向って最後の一蹴りをする意志の力をもまたどこにも見出さないだろう！曾祖父の弟や鷹四はかれらの死を目前にしてそのようではなかった、かれらは自分たちの地獄を確認し、「本当の事」を叫んでそれを乗りこえたのだ。 (442)

> Since I had not found out the "truth" myself, I would not be able to find anywhere the power of will to make a final leap toward death. It hadn't been like that with great-grand-father's brother and Takashi just before they died: they had been sure of their own hell, and in crying out the "truth" had risen above it. (270)[14]

The "truth" for Taka is included in his last confession to Mitsu that he has committed incest with their younger sister, who later killed herself. Of course, we can here hear the echo of Quentin in *The Sound and the Fury*, who on the last day of his life imagines himself confessing to his father that he has committed incest with Caddy. But the "truth" for Taka is not so much the incestuous desire, narcissism, the Oedipus complex, or the castration complex, as seen in the psychoanalytic Quentin, as the fact that his later careless, or even cruel, attitudes toward his sister led her to her suicide. While Quentin's lament for the loss of his sister is, following psychoanalytic readings, symbolic, Taka's is ethical. What is important for Taka, therefore, is to confess his sin, and also compensate for his sister's death. The ultimate "truth" for Taka is his compensatory death. In

other words, in his own death does Taka find his "truth," that is, what
Faulkner calls "*is*." For Taka, though paradoxically, death is his life
within.

Such a leap toward life, however, is Taka's longtime wish. It does
not even originate from his sister's suicide. When Taka meets Mitsu
after his return from America, Taka has already suggested to Mitsu
that he had had a wish to leap even before he committed incest with
his sister:

> 「僕は、いまや死の匂いのするものに、すっかりと
> りかこまれてしまった模様だよ」
> 「もし、そうだとしたら、蜜、それをふりきって生
> の領域にのぼってこなければならない。そうしなけれ
> ば死の匂いが蜜にうつるよ」
> 「アメリカで、きみは迷信家の精神を獲得してきた
> のかね」
> 「その通りだ」と弟は、僕がかれの言葉によって僕
> の内部の空洞にもたらされた反響を隠蔽しようとして
> いるのを見すかして追討ちをかけてきた。「しかし、お
> れは子供のころに色濃く持っていて、その後たまたま
> 放棄していたそういう精神を、あらためてもういちど、
> ひろいあげたにすぎないよ。妹とおれが草の家を作っ
> てしばらくそこで暮したのを覚えていないか？あの時
> おれたちは、死の匂いから遠ざかろうとして、新生活
> をやっていたんだよ。あれは、S兄さんが撲り殺され
> たすぐあとのことだからね」(65)

"I seem to be surrounded by the odor of death," I said.

"If that's so, Mitsu, then shake yourself free and climb up
into the world of the living again. Otherwise the odor will
rub off on you."

"Does that mean you've picked up the superstitious
mentality in America?" I said.

"That's right," my brother went on relentlessly, seeing

through my attempt to obscure the echoes his words had set up in the void within me. "But all I've done in fact is take up again something that was very marked in me when I was a kid and that I happened to put aside later in life. Remember how sister and I built a thatched hut and lived there for a while? We were starting a new life, trying to get away from the smell of mortality. It was just after S was beaten to death, as you know." (34–35)

Like Quentin in *The Sound and the Fury*, who is haunted by death, Taka has been haunted by death even before his sister's suicide. Her death only brings Taka back to the "odor of death," from which he tried to separate her and himself by building a "thatched hut" together. Since then, or even before that, Taka has been living a deathly life, the exact opposite of Faulkner's "*is*," a life which collapses death. By telling the "truth," however, Taka finally gets over such a deathly life. For Taka, suicide is not a way of death, but rather a leap back to life.

Similarly, we can interpret Quentin's suicide as his final leap to get over a life haunted by death. Faulkner wrote in the "Appendix" in *The Portable Faulkner* that Quentin loved death (743). We can take this as Faulkner's own inquiry into the last moment of Quentin's life. The "Appendix" suggests that Quentin killed himself not because he was haunted by death but because he loved death. Paradoxically, for Quentin, death is not death as such, but rather a way of life. His suicide is not to become "*was*," but to become "*is*." As a matter of fact, his memory lives in Caddy, who names her daughter Quentin. Similarly, Taka lives in Mitsu as "*is*." In the last paragraph of *The Silent Cry*, Mitsu expresses his decision to go to Africa. Oe seems deliberately to reverse the meaning of the return of the repressed in *Absalom, Absalom!* Going to Africa is a way for Mitsu to remember Taka and make a leap toward a new life. For Quentin, the return of Henry—the repressed—forms a repetition or doubling. For Mitsu, on the other hand, the return of the Taka in himself prepares a way to reject such a repetition.

Accepting two children is another way for Mitsu to make the leap. One simple way to see a leap in Mitsu's acceptance of two children is to take it as an antithesis to the ending of *Absalom, Absalom!* in which Jim Bond, the mentally deficient grandson of Charles Bon, is left as the only descendent of Thomas Sutpen, and after the fire that kills Henry and Clytie, disappears. Fowler equates Jim Bond with the repressed itself; therefore, Fowler argues, he himself does not have the subject that is formed by the void made by repression. According to Fowler, Jim Bond is at the same time the "last one" in a "novel, which is filled with forbidden, unrecognized images out of the unconsciousness," and "another formulation of our desire to return, both to return the repressed and to return to the origin" (*Faulkner* 126–27). In the psychoanalytic reading, the repressed, the last one, means death; in this sense, Shreve at the end of the novel has aptly expressed the psychoanalytic idea of death, that is, that we all, not only individually but also as a whole civilization, wish to return to death:

> I think that in time the Jim Bonds are going to conquer the western hemisphere. Of course it wont quite be in our time and of course as they spread toward the poles they will bleach out again like the rabbits and the birds do, so they wont show up so sharp against the snow. But it will still be Jim Bond; and so in a few thousand years, I who regard you will also have sprung from the loins of African kings. (Faulkner, *Absalom, Absalom!* 302)

Apart from Shreve's intentional use of racist expressions (Fowler, *Faulkner* 125–26), this passage implies that in our origin—the repressed, or death—is our end, and in our end—the repressed, death—our beginning.

In a sense, *The Silent Cry* fits this pattern of repetition, since it ends with Mitsu's return home, or return to the Taka in himself. Both children are Taka's doubles; for Mitsu, they represent what he has denied, or repressed. By accepting them, Mitsu symbolically tries to begin a new life with what he has always had: that is, in his beginning is his end, and his end is his beginning. This is exactly what Freud suggested in his essay, "The Uncanny": what is uncanny—*unheimlich*, in German—is originally something most intimate or hidden— *heimlich*. However, this does not explain why Oe needed two children to end his novel. Neither does it clarify the leap that Mitsu has made, or decides to make, at the end of the novel.

To understand Mitsu's acceptance of two children at the end of *The Silent Cry*, we have to know that this is not actually the ending but rather the beginning of a series of novels in which Oe repeatedly uses the motif of a pair that is spiritually united: to name the most obvious, Mori-father and Mori in *Pinchi ranna chosho* (*The Pinch Runner Memorandum*), "I" and sister in *Dojidai gemu*, "I" and Brother Gii in *Natsukashii toshi e no tegami*, Michio and Musan in *Jinsei no shinseki* (*An Echo of Heaven*), "I" and Brother Gii in *Moeagaru midori no ki*, and Guide and Patron in *Chugaeri* (*Somersault*). The similar pair, however, can be seen even before *The Silent Cry* in "I" and brother in "Shiiku," and Yasuo and his brother Shigeru in *Warera no jidai* (Our Age, 1959); especially, in the latter, we can see the, so-to-speak, type to be realized by its antitype in the relationship between Mitsu and Taka in *The Silent Cry*.

In *Warera no jidai,* Yasuo, a university student, spends days purposelessly, finding solace in the relationship with his girl friend Yoriko, who is a whore, while hoping to flee from the situation, which he calls *jigoku* (hell) or *eigokaiki* (eternal recurrence of the same); on the other hand, his brother Shigeru, a jazz pianist, is planning to go gypsying around the world with his band "Unlucky Young Men." Yasuo's essay, which he wrote for the competition sponsored by French publisher and Japanese newspaper office, gets the first prize and Yasuo gets a chance to leave Japan for France; on the other hand, in the pursuit by the police after the accidental death of two other members of the band, Shigeru dies also accidentally by falling from the window of Yasuo's Algerian friend's room. Asked by the secretary of the French embassy about his relation to the Algerian friend, Yasuo expresses his support for the political movement in Algeria, and loses his chance to go to France. At the end of the novel, after losing everything including Yoriko, Yasuo thinks that committing suicide is the only way out of his purposeless life. He tries to jump from the bridge into a coming train, only to find himself unable to make the final leap.

The similarity between *Warera no jidai* and *The Silent Cry* seems clear: in both novels, after the death of younger brother, the protagonist faces a Hamlet-like question of whether to leap or not to leap. However, the difference between two novels also seems clear: *Warera no jidai* lacks—it seem to be the novel's defect—the inner connection between the younger brother's death and the protagonist's final decision or indecision, while *The Silent Cry* centers on interaction between two brothers to the final decision made by the protagonist after his brother's death. Moreover, there is another important motif that separates *The Silent Cry* from *Warera no jidai*: that is, the motif of pregnancy, abortion, or new life. In *Warera no jidai*, Yoriko becomes pregnant by Yasuo, but after simply shocking him, she wants an abortion of her own choice. Also, after unintentionally kicking a pregnant cat in her belly and aborting her, Shigeru says to his brother that he hates pregnancy, and Yasuo agrees. *Warera no jidai* is filled with such curses against sex, pregnancy, and life itself. As seen above, the ending of *The Silent Cry* turns the tables: Mitsu decides to retrieve his son from the institution and also accepts Taka's child in his wife's belly.

In 1963, Oe's first son was born with a serious deformity in his head; in 1964, Oe's friend killed himself in Paris. Obviously, these two incidents had a decisive influence on the writing of *The Silent Cry*. In the novel, Oe's son becomes Mitsu's mentally deficient son, and Oe's friend the friend of Mitsu and Taka, who hanged himself with his head painted crimson and a cucumber thrust in his anus. At the last meeting with the friend in New York, Taka "had seen into something essential in my friend's mind" (17) 友人の核心にふれた

(35). For Mitsu, Taka is the friend reincarnated and Taka's child both Taka and the friend combined and reincarnated. To accept Taka's child in his wife's belly, therefore, means for Mitsu to live with both Taka and his friend. For Oe, in this sense, two children at the end of the novel were a necessary means to do a kind of double homage to his own son and friend, and at the same time give a form to his idea of leap. What is seen at the end of *The Silent Cry* becomes the prototype of the leap to be reenacted repeatedly in Oe's later novels, and his own life as well. For example, *Somersault* is one of its manifestations. When his friend Takemitsu died in 1996, Oe decided to take back his earlier decision to break the pencil and leap into another phase of his writing. This is an intentional reenactment of the relationship between Mitsu and Taka in *The Silent Cry*.

Originally, Oe got the idea of leap from a poem "Leap Before You Look" by W. H. Auden, one of the favorite poets of his early days. In his early short story "Miru mae ni tobe" (Leap Before You Look, 1958), which features a university student who, just like Yasuo in *Warera no jidai*, goes through the question of Algeria, a relationship with a whore, and his girl friend's abortion, and finally falls into the sense of inertia or inability to leap, Oe quotes a line from the poem: "Look if you like, but you will have to leap." For Oe, writing *The Silent Cry* was such a leap, that is, a leap into a new phase in his writing career. Similarly, for Mitsu, accepting children is such a leap into a new phase of his own life. It is his "*is*," that is, the way through which Taka keeps moving in his heart.

Metaphorical Doubling: Snopes and "The Day He Himself Shall Wipe My Tears Away"

As Lothar Hönnighausen argues, as an heir to Willa Cather's and Sherwood Anderson's regionalism and also T. S. Eliot's modernism, Faulkner wears the masks of both, and "employs metaphor to achieve the fusion of the regional with the universal" (232). In the interview with Jean Stein, Faulkner himself described such a metaphorical "fusion of the regional and the universal" as "sublimating the actual into apocryphal" (Meriwether and Millgate 255). Perhaps, among all Faulknerian terms, the apocryphal best explains the political function of Oe's fictional village. Joseph Urgo stresses that Faulkner's Yoknapatawpha is not "mythical" but "apocryphal": "In Cowley's view, Faulkner's 'mythical' world of Yoknapatawpha 'explained' something—the South, its history, its people. To Faulkner, his 'apocryphal' vision offered an alternative view to something which, without the apocrypha, would be taken for granted as real" (*Faulkner's Apocrypha* 15). Urgo also informs us that the root meaning of the word apocrypha is "hidden, concealed, obscure" (31). As we have seen with "'Ame no ki' o kiku onnatachi," for Oe, metaphor is a way to glimpse what is repressed or hidden. To create his own Yoknapatawpha, then, means for Oe to glimpse the universal hidden in the regional. In other words, for Oe, Faulkner's Yoknapatawpha is an attempt to let the true universal stand out against the false universal that has been authoritatively, but falsely, called universal. Drawing on Faulkner's Yoknapatawpha, Oe's fictional village contains such subversive intentions.

However, Oe's metaphorical exploration into the regional is not an appeal to the uniqueness of a regional truth against the already established universal truth. Rather, it is an attempt to deconstruct the hierarchy between the regional and the universal, the marginal and the central, the hidden and the established. Oe's attempt, then, is what Sarah Kofman describes as Nietzschean:

> Tyranny is reprehensible in all its forms, including that of
> any philosopher seeking to raise his spontaneous evaluation
> to the status of an absolute value and his style to that of a
> philosophical style 'in itself,' opposed to poetic style 'in
> itself' like truth opposed to untruth, good to evil. But the
> tyranny of anyone seeking simply to invert the terms and
> commend the value of metaphor alone is equally repre-
> hensible: he remains ensnared in the same system of

thought as the metaphysician. Whether writing is conceptual
or metaphorical (and since Nietzsche the opposition has
hardly applied any longer), the essential thing is to be able
to laugh at it, to be at enough of a distance from it to make
fun of it. (3)

Oe's fictional village is supposed to have as its keystone "*is*," that is,
the idea of time which sees human immortality as existent in the
mortality of each "momentary avatar." If so, it resembles Japan,
which is said to have miraculously recovered from the ruins of war, as
if it had proven its immortality through the presence of the Emperor,
who is believed to be transmitted through ages. From the point of
view of such a shared ambition for immortality, the distinction
between Japan and Oe's village disappears. Oe's village, then, becomes Japan's metaphorical—or, to be more precise, metonymical—
double.

For Oe, however, as Kofman puts it, the "essential thing is to be
able to laugh at it, to be at enough of a distance from it to make fun of
it." Metaphorically juxtaposed with Japan, Oe's fictional village blurs
the boundary between the regional and the universal, the marginal and
the central, and also the royal and the vulgar. To cause that blur, Oe
uses Bakhtin's method of grotesque realism. In *Shosetsu no hoho*, Oe
summarizes the method as follows;

　《グロテスク・リアリズムの主要な特質は、格下げ・
下落であって、高位のもの、精神的、理想的、抽象的
なものをすべて物質的・肉体的次元へと移行させるこ
とである。この大地と肉の次元は切り離し難い一つの
統一体となっている。》
　《格下げ・引き落としとはこの際地上的なものに向
かうこと、一切を飲みこみ、それと同時に生み出す原
理としての大地と一体化させることを意味する。つま
り格下げ・下落させつつ、埋葬し、同時に播種し、殺
すのであるが、それは新たにより良くより大きな形で

生むためなのである。》 (212)

> The principle characteristic of grotesque realism lies in degradation and lowering; it transfers everything highranking, spiritual, ideal, abstract into the material and carnal. The dimension of earth and flesh forms an indivisible unit.
>
> Degradation and lowering mean, in this case, to move toward the earthly, to at once engulf and incorporate everything into the earth as the principle of giving birth. That is, degradation and lowering lead to burying, seeding, killing, only to re-create anew the degraded and lowered in a better and bigger form. (my translation)

As a metaphorical counterpart, Oe's fictional village degrades and lowers Japan's spiritual value that is symbolized by the Emperor. Oe's village, in this sense, is a strategic double metaphor for two different, but look-alike, space-time continuums, in both of which time is similarly in a fluid condition. However, we should not even expect a difference here, since, as Oe says, degradation and lowering serve only to re-create anew the degraded and lowered in a better and bigger form. Strategically, Oe's village is meant to involve both itself and Japan into one and the same process of re-creation.[15]

Even before Oe defines them in *Shosetsu no hoho*, degradation and lowering have already been practiced in *The Silent Cry*, especially in its title that literally means "football in the first year of *Man'en*." *Man'en* is the name of an era (1860–1861) in the periodization system peculiar to Japan, which names each Emperor's reign. In a lecture given in San Francisco in 1990, Oe calls the attention of the audience to such a peculiar sense of time:

> The modern nation-state of Japan continues to mark the passage of time by using names for eras whose currency holds good in Japan alone, names such as Meiji (1868–1912), Taisho (1912–1925), and Showa (1925–1989). And

the Showa Emperor's death in 1989 revealed the power of
this metaphorical system, wherein the names given to eras
change with the passing of an emperor, resulting in a widely
shared impression among the general public that a distinct
period had come to an end. ("On Modern and Contemporary
Japanese Literature" 42–43)

Oe describes the periodization system peculiar to Japanese, and the
emperor system that supports it, as "metaphorical." In the title of the
novel, "football" is also a metaphor, or metonymy, for America. In the
novel, Taka plays American football with his followers to stir up their
morale in looting the supermarket owned by the "Emperor of the
supermarkets." Before Taka's leap—another metaphor—invokes a
new sense of time in Mitsu, such metaphors as the "Emperor of the
supermarkets" and "football" humorously describe the situation in
which they—and Japanese—are entrapped. It is the political situation
of Japan around 1960, in which, on the one hand, Japan is eco-
nomically already on the rise under the American nuclear umbrella
(American-type supermarket leads the village economy), but not yet
recovered from the sense of loss and shame caused by the defeat of
World War II (the "Emperor of the supermarkets" is Korean), and
on the other hand, the leftist student activists, who oppose U.S.-
Japan Security Treaty, love, or at least have already naturalized, the
American looks or the American way of life (Taka plays American
football). This is an image of Japan around 1960, in which no one can
or should any longer be purely rightist or leftist, ideally traditional or
liberal.

Oe's return to his native village is from the beginning a
metaphorical gesture against the centripetal tendency in Japanese
culture and politics in the 1950s and 1960s. The incident that
decisively motivated Oe to create his own apocryphal world in
opposition to the mainstream, authoritarian Japan was the assas-
sination of Asanuma Inejiro, the chairman of the Socialist Party,
by a seventeen-year-old right-winger, Yamaguchi Otoya, in 1960.

Yamaguchi stabbed Asanuma to death, while he was on stage for a speech, and later killed himself. For Oe, this incident was shocking because Yamaguchi seemed to have succeeded in unifying himself with the Emperor in a flawless ultranationalistic vision. Oe calls this terrorism an "epiphany, or the moment when something formless was suddenly materialized before our eyes" (my translation); エピファニ ーというか、形のないものが、一挙に目の前に具体化される瞬間 (Oe and Subaru Henshuubu 67). Since then, what Oe has attempted through his fictional village is to present a counter-vision to the visionary ultranationalism in which every Japanese is integrated into one body, a god incarnate, who is the Emperor. Oe's fictional village, which is linked to a transcendental vision of its own, is his attempt to leap out of such an imagined community called Japan. Oe's aim, however, is not so much to separate himself from Japan as to see them in a whole process of re-creation. In other words, for Oe, it is not enough just to throw an ironical look from outside. Rather, he wants to laugh.

We can see a similar attitude in Faulkner. It is generally assumed that there is a transition in Faulkner's career from the earlier modernistic, nostalgic, image-oriented style to the later, more relaxed, prospective, story-oriented style. However, it is more than just a transition, since the latter not only replaces the former but also appears as a reformation of the former or even its dissolution into a higher level. When Richard C. Moreland distinguishes humor, which is seen in "Barn Burning," *The Hamlet*, *Go Down Moses*, *Requiem for a Nun* and *The Reivers*, from irony seen in *Absalom, Absalom!*, *The Unvanquished* and *If I Forget Thee, Jerusalem*, he seems to be making the same point. Moreland asserts that contrary to irony which appears as "compulsive repetition," humor appears as "revisionary repetition," which "repeats some structured event, in order somehow to alter that structure and its continuing power, especially by opening a critical space for what the subject might learn about that structure in the different context or a changing present or a more distant or different past" (4). To apply Moreland here, we can say that Oe's village is a "revisionary repetition" of Japan by way of metaphors. For Oe, it should not be a "compulsive repetition," which sounds as if he could not but return to Japan. Oe's challenge is to take Japan out into a metaphorical space and dissolve it into a cosmos of his own, which is in itself a metaphor for the general metaphoricity of every imagined community.

In this sense, Theresa M. Towner's speculation on the metaphoricity of race in Faulkner's later novels is important. Drawing on Henry Louis Gates, Jr., Towner points out the general artificiality, fictionality, or metaphoricity, of race in the later Faulkner: "'Race' and 'art' thus become, in Faulkner's later career, functions of one another" (8); "Gates notes that scientifically speaking, 'race' is a fiction, a term that 'pretends to be an objective term of classification, when in fact it is a dangerous trope" (10–11); "Faulkner's work might not be 'about' race, but it is always about 'race'" (11). For Oe, too, his village is not only a metaphor for Japan but also a metaphor for the general metaphoricity of Japan as imagined community. Following Towner, we can say that Oe's novels which present a Yoknapatawpha-like literary microcosm are not "about" Japan, but are always about "Japan" the metaphor. In Oe, we can see the same transition as seen in Faulkner, that is, from irony to humor, and also from Japan to "Japan."[16]

In Oe's career, what corresponds to the earlier Faulkner is Oe's literary, ten-year older rival, Mishima Yukio. In 1970, Mishima killed himself by *seppuku* after breaking into the Ichigaya headquarters of Japan Self-Defense Forces with other four members of *Tate no kai*, or the Shield Society, Mishima's own private army. Taking the commander as hostage, and delivering a speech from the balcony of the building, in which he insisted on the restoration of the true Japanese or *samurai* spirit, Mishima acted out the behavior he thought should be embodied by the Self-Defense Forces. Mishima himself did not expect to be heard physically; his voice was soon drowned by shouts from below and the sounds of helicopters from above. Later, Oe labels Mishima's attempt *feiku*, or fake (Oe and Subaru

Henshuubu 67). Oe sees in Mishima a sense of irony toward ultra-nationalism.[17] In this sense, Oe is not necessarily negative about Mishima, although he is often taken as such, since Mishima's irony is his own. Mishima's irony was targeted at the ultranationalism which he himself represented; in Oe's case, irony is directed toward the democracy of post-World War II Japan. Although Oe has been an earnest advocate of democracy throughout his life, he describes post-World War II Japan as a gilded age. In the sense that they share an ironical stance toward the political or even spiritual condition of post-World War II Japan, Oe and Mishima are allies.

Oe was even aware of that alignment, when he published "The Day He Himself Shall Wipe My Tears Away" in October 1971 as an immediate response to Mishima's suicide. As we have seen at the beginning of this chapter, Oe has revealed his debt to Faulkner's Snopes trilogy in writing it. This novella is a product of the same four or five years of Oe's intensive reading of Faulkner (perhaps from 1966 through 1971), out of which *The Silent Cry* also emerged. The novella also features Oe's fictional native village.

In the novella, "he" narrates to his wife the story of the days of good relationship with his father, that is, "Happy Days," and tries to let her believe that "he" is inheriting in himself the spirit of his father. At the end of World War II, "he"'s father tried to attack the Emperor's palace with other soldiers and paradoxically protect the glory of the Emperor by killing him. Throughout, "he" keeps calling his father *ano hito* あの人, or He, meaning both his father and the Emperor.[18] Since "he" was deeply influenced by his father through those "Happy Days" (that is, the period of about three years between 1942 and 1945), and has become a fervent admirer of the Emperor like his father, he cannot distinguish between his father and the Emperor. Later in the short story, his mother reveals to both him and his wife that his father was killed a day after the war ended in an attempt to rob a bank, not at the end of the war in a heroic attempt to die a martyr to the Emperor's honor. Nevertheless, he still tries to believe that "At the moment of his death, He leaped beyond the limits of His individuality, becoming a gold chrysanthemum flower of 675,000 square kilometers, embellished by a purple aurora, at the height where He can cover the entire territory of Japan" (my translation); あの人は、その死の瞬間に個人の限界を跳びだして、やはり紫色のオーロラにかざられた、六十七万五千平方キロメートルの黄金の菊の花を、日本全領土をすっぽりおおいつくす位置にあらわしたのだ (Oe, "Mizukara" 127–28). A chrysanthemum is the crest of the Japanese Imperial Family. "He" here means both his father and the Emperor. Here, Oe intentionally tries to imitate an ultranationalistic vision of Japan as presided over by the transcendental image of the immortal emperorship, in which the Emperor and his every subject unite beyond each individual level. By so doing, Oe is trying to mock an ultranationalistic consciousness that prevailed during World War II.

There is, however, more at stake here. "He," the son, is both Mishima and Oe himself; moreover, the relationship between his father and "he" can be taken as that between Mishima and Oe himself. "He," the father, can mean, therefore, his father, the Emperor, and also Mishima. By integrating all of them into one patriarchal order and mysteriously calling it "He," Oe points out his own conspirational relationship with them all. As a matter of fact, we can no longer distinguish between the transcendental level that the metaphor of a chrysanthemum represents in this short story and that which such metaphors as *"ame no ki," Kowasuhito, mori no fushigi,* and *natsukashii toshi* represent in Oe's later novels. What we see here is Oe's self-criticism, or a preemptive criticism of the repetition of ultra-nationalistic images, patriarchal structure, or the idea of immortality, which his coming novels will inevitably facilitate.

Now, we can finally understand how significant the Snopes trilogy was for Oe to write "The Day He Himself Shall Wipe My Tears Away," since the influence is concerned with the central metaphor, "He." It is rather easy to point out that, like the boldfaced *Kowasuhito* in *Dojidai gemu, ano hito* ("He") is also boldfaced in the original Japanese text, in the manner, according to Oe, that *"they, them, it"* in *The Mansion* is italicized to cause in the minds of readers

a sense of unfamiliarity. In *The Mansion*, *"they, them, it"* represents
some God-like being, in which Mink believes:

> He had simply had to trust *them*—the *Them* of whom it was
> promised that not even a sparrow should fall unmarked. By
> *them* he didn't mean that whatever-it-was that folks referred
> to as Old Moster. He didn't believe in any Old Moster. He
> had seen too much in his time that, if any Old Moster
> existed, with eyes as sharp and power as strong as was
> claimed He had, He would have done something about. (5)

In spite of his disbelief in what is called God or "Old Moster," Mink
still believes in what *"they, them, it"* represents, that is, what he thinks
"fundamental justice and equity in human affairs" (6). For Mink, like
Oe's *"ame no ki,"* *"they, them, it"* is the metaphor for the ultimate
order in the cosmos in which he lives. To Mink, however, *"they, them,
it"* is not congenial. On the contrary, *"they, them, it"* "harass and
worry him," or "even just sit back and watch everything go against
him right along without missing a lick, almost like there was a pattern
to it." The only and best means that Mink has learned to deal with
"they, them, it" is to wait. Mink has learned it through a series of hard
lessons, such as: he waits for a whole winter to get his cow back from
Jack Houston, only to get insulted; he kills Houston, while Flem is
absent, because he "could wait no longer" (5); he waits for Flem, in
vain, to come to help him out of jail; he waits for his term to end, but
seduced by Montgomery Ward, escapes and gets another term; he
waits in jail for the total period of thirty eight years to finally take
revenge on Flem; even in front of his target, he has to trigger twice to
shoot his only bullet and serve his purpose. The moment he kills Flem,
Mink finally meets what he has waited for, that is, what *"they, them,
it"* represents. That is, for Mink, meeting and killing Flem cannot be
distinguished from meeting *"they, them, it."* Ultimately, for Mink,
"they, them, it" appears as Flem. This resembles the imagined
moment in "The Day He Himself Shall Wipe My Tears Away" when

"he"'s father could have killed the Emperor. At that moment, "He," "he"'s father, was supposed to be united with another "He," the Emperor. Like "*they, them, it*" in *The Mansion*, "He" in Oe's short story represents both a transcendental, godlike, being, and the more immediate, earthly being as the focus of the central character's attention.

The scene of Mink's killing Flem climaxes the story of Flem's rise that has been narrated through the trilogy. It is the culmination of not only Mink's waiting but also the whole process of Snopes-watching, in which Flem is always at the center. As "he"'s father is the focus of "he"'s narration in "The Day He Himself Shall Wipe My Tears Away," Flem, who rarely speaks, is the mysterious center of the whole narration of the trilogy. On the metaphorical level, "he"'s father and the Emperor are identical; similarly, Flem and "*they, them, it*" are identical. So far, we can see that in "The Day He Himself Shall Wipe My Tears Away" Oe borrowed from the Snopes trilogy the use of metaphor which represents both a godlike being and its human embodiment. However, Oe draws more from the trilogy by adding Mishima to his metaphor of "He." By hinting Mishima by the metaphor of "He," Oe transfers the relationship between "he," the fictional narrator, and "He" into the relationship between he himself and Mishima. Then, "He" is no longer a mere metaphor for "he"'s father or the Emperor, but becomes a metaphor for the ubiquitous presence of Mishima in Oe's every novel and short story. Now, what is important for Oe is no longer "*they, them, it*" in *The Mansion*, but the relationship between the metaphoricity of Flem or "*they, them, it*" and the whole narration of the trilogy. That is, the Snopes trilogy itself is no longer "about" Flem, but about "Flem." In other words, as a whole, the Snopes trilogy is not so much centered on Flem, a person, as it reveals the metaphoricity of a character called "Flem."

Oe's literary endeavors have apparently focused on the criticism of Mishima's irony directed toward the political and spiritual situations of post-World War II Japan. Mishima's irony has ended up entailing, on the one hand, an intentionally acquired innocence which denies the present and idealizes the past, and, on the other hand, a series of convulsive reenactments of the traumatic scene of failed attempt to become one with the transcendentalized ideal. In "The Day He Himself Shall Wipe My Tears Away," Oe purposely repeats Mishima's ironical stance toward ultranationalism. *Dojidai gemu, M/T to mori no fushigi no monogatari,* and *Natsukashii toshi eno tegami* follow such an attempt. In those novels in which he creates his own Yoknapatawpha, Oe attempts to present a strategic double of the ultranationalistic Japan. His own Yoknapatawpha in those later novels, in this sense, reflects Oe's intentional repetition of Mishima's irony.

Oe admits that he "has tried to suppress in [his] unconscious the fact that [he] is a person who is easily drawn to ultranationalism, or even strongly attracted by it" (my translation); 超国家主義的なものに引きずられやすい、それに強い魅力を感じる人間だということは、無意識の中に押さえ込もうとしていた (Oe and Subaru Henshuubu 66). Through his fictional village, or, to be more precise, the fictionality of his fictional village, however, Oe has already revealed the fictionality of such an ultranationalism hidden in himself. Then Oe is not even ironical about his own ultranationalism. On the contrary, Oe laughs at it. We can see here another parallel between Faulkner and Oe. Faulkner's notorious interview with Russell Howe, for example, has been bothering us with a question: was Faulkner a racist?[19] Towner writes, however: "the question 'Was Faulkner a racist?' is not only unanswerable but also a kind of hermeneutic red herring. . . . 'Faulkner's' racial persona is traceable only in the language he uses to serve the moment" (121). If we can say, as we have already said, that Faulkner is always metaphorical, or apocryphal, we should rather ask: Was "Faulkner" a racist? By intentionally repeating Mishima's irony, Oe is not so much writing about Mishima as metaphorically doubling Mishima or metaphorically expressing a Mishima in himself.[20] In other words, Oe is trying to turn himself into a metaphor for Mishima. By so doing, Oe tries to dissolve Mishima's irony into his humorous repetitions and to laugh at it.

Oe's own Yoknapatawpha thus entails a criticism against the

Emperor-centered Japan, or the ultranationalistic view of Japan's immortality. As we will see in Chapter Two, however, Oe's criticism of Japan is not yet sufficient without a criticism against his own presence as male novelist. For Oe, the male "I" in his own novels appears as the chief enemy which represents the Emperor-centered, patriarchal Japan. It is not until the end of the 1980s, however, that Oe finally gets to the self-criticism which involves a revision of his habitual male first-person narration. Moreover, in Chapter Three, we will see Oe's criticism of the idea of immortality. There, we will see a curious connection between Faulkner's *A Fable* and Oe's own, most recent Yoknapatawpha novel, *Chugaeri (Somersault)*. As Faulkner opposes human spirit, or *"is,"* to the idea of immortality, Oe opposes soul to immortality. Through the opposition, or the apparent resemblance between the two, Oe again tries to laugh at the whole ambiguity. In *Somersault*, however, Oe seems pessimistic.

Notes

1. See *Shosetsu no takurami, chi no tanoshimi* (50–53, 154–59), *Watashi to iu shosetsuka no tsukurikata* (43–44), *Shosetsu no keiken* (65–73), and *Iigataki nageki mote* (164).

2. For the idea of duration, see especially Chapter II of Bergson's *Time and Free Will: An Essay on the Immediate Data of Consciousness*. Studies of the Bergsonian time in Faulkner abound. For the recent discussions, see, for example, Mortimer (43–71), Gidley (377–83), Douglass (142–65), Slaughter (65–84), Rio-Jelliffe (19–73). O'Donnell's 2003 article on Faulkner's (or Giorgio Agamben's) "modern condition," in which "our experience of time and event passing at ever greater speed, to the point at which everything seems instantaneous, a matter of the split second, is out of sync with our concept of history as a succession of events that can be placed into diachronic orders and hierarchies" (110) can be also regarded as another expression of the Bergsonian duration in Faulkner.

3. Mortimer (1983) points out that Faulkner himself metaphorically

translates Bergson's conception of time into visual examples (52–54). Mortimer writes: "A second way in which Faulkner describes motion obliquely rather than directly is to use metaphorical language that compares it with *other* motion. This device has the same effect as the creation of tableaux; it obviates the necessity of using active verbs and of narratively depicting the continuity of action in itself. Perhaps his intention is to avoid describing as if it were objectively real what Faulkner (with Bergson) believes to be essentially an illusion, the notion of continuity" (52).

4. In the interview with Loïc Bouvard, Faulkner suggests that the ultimate metaphor for "*is*" is God. Asked if he is talking about the "God of Bergson," Faulkner answers yes. See Meriwether and Millgate 70.

5. Throughout *Dojidai gemu*, *Kowasuhito* 壊す人 is boldfaced. Enomoto suggests that Oe borrowed that method from the Snopes trilogy: in an essay published in March 1981, Oe writes that the italics of "*they, them, it*" in *The Mansion* "brings to our consciousness the sense of something unfamiliar"; われわれの意識に異物感をもたらす (qtd. in Enomoto 57).

6. Yoshida Sanroku's decription of *Kowasuhito* is interesting: "It is possible that the 'Destroyer' is the embodiment of 'entropy,' the theory that the amount of disorder in the cosmos only increases as time passes. This is paradoxical in that one cannot keep creating without destroying what one has just created; in the final analysis, the figure of the 'Destroyer' is a metaphorical composite both abstract and concrete, provoking a sense of ambiguity and ambivalence" (93).

7. Letter to Joan Williams (7 Aug. 1952), quoted in Blotner (1431) and Minter (224).

8. In "'Ame no ki' o kiku onnatachi," in which "I" asks his friend to translate the definition of the "rain tree" into English, the word "ingenious" is used for the word which is supposed to be *atama no ii* 頭のいい (35). It should be noted, however, no original Japanese sentence is given in the text. We cannot even know if the short story mentioned in "'Ame no ki' o kiku onnatachi" is "Atama no ii 'Ame no ki.'" The German title of "Atama no ii 'Ame no ki'" is "Der Kluge Regenbaum."

9. T is modeled on Takemitsu Toru (1930–1996) and the piece is "Rain Tree"

(Premiere, May 1981).

10. Oe quotes the line from *Faulkner in the University* (25). In the novel, *If I Forget Thee, Jerusalem*, the corresponding sentence is: "*Between grief and nothing I will take grief*" (273).

11. I have argued elsewhere that the relationship between Mitsu and Taka is the combination of the relationship between Quentin and Shreve and that between Quentin and Henry. See my article, "*Absalom, Absalom!* and *Man'en gannen no futtoboru.*"

12. All references to the original *Man'en gannen no futtoboru* in this study are to Oe Kenzaburo, *Man'en gannen no futtoboru* (Tokyo: Kodansha, 1988). For the translation, I used John Bester's—Oe Kenzaburo, *The Silent Cry* (Tokyo: Kodansha International, 1974)—, unless otherwise noted.

13. In "Revising *The Sound and the Fury*: *Absalom, Absalom!* and Faulkner's Postmodern Turn," Fowler asserts that the scene of Quentin's encounter with Henry reads as an image in which, merging with Henry's, Quentin's identity breaks down, and through the image Quentin reaches a kind of postmodern awareness that "identity and meaning are human constructions" (106). I would suggest that this is another way of explaining how Quentin's identity coheres with Henry's, or how Quentin gets involved in repetition, doubling, and the recurring fate.

14. The translation of the first sentence is mine. Bester translated it as "If I hadn't yet grasped the 'truth,' I was unlikely to find the strength of purpose to take that final plunge into death" (270). *Ishi no chikara* 意志の力 sounds like Nietzschean term *chikara eno ishi* 力への意志, which corresponds to "will to power," and *saigo no hitokeri* 最後の一蹴り is related to the idea of leap.

15. For a discussion of Oe's use of Bakhtin's grotesque realism, see Wilson 96–104.

16. Urgo (2001) insists that "Yoknapatawpha County and thereabouts is Faulkner's performance of America" (99). Similarly, we can say that Oe's own Yoknapatawpha is his performance of Japan.

17. For Oe's own comments on Mishima's irony, see Oe and Subaru Henshuubu 61–68.

18. *Ano hito* literally means "that person."

19. See, especially, Meriwether and Millgate 260–61.

20. Susan J. Napier points out that the "fictionality" (167), "stylistic complexity" (168), and "artistry" (171) of "The Day He Himself Shall Wipe My Tears Away" are intentionally posited against Mishima's "confusion of the 'word' with 'action,' of the fictional with the real" (168). Napier also appreciates Mishima's irony, by pointing out the "sense of betrayal" which is "so beautifully and movingly rendered [in Mishima's short story, "Eirei no koe" (Hero Spirits)] that Mishima's attitude towards the emperor remains problematic" (174). Nevertheless, Napier basically assumes that both Oe's and Mishima's "yearning for a 'concentrated life' is a genuine one" (172). In a sense, Napier is right, since Oe himself admits that. However, in spite of her understanding of "fictionality," Napier seems to be making the same mistake as one who literally calls Faulkner a racist.

Chapter Two

The Feminine

Oe's Feminist Turn

While it seems rather obvious that Faulkner's earlier Yokna-patawpha novels, especially *The Sound and the Fury*, *Absalom, Absalom!*, and *Go Down, Moses*, influenced Oe, the influence of Faulkner's later novels on Oe has been generally neglected, in spite of Oe's own frequent reference to the Snopes trilogy, especially *The Town*. This neglect is related to two other neglects: first, it has been overlooked that Oe experiences a feminist turn in the 1980s, or what we also call in the argument below, borrowing Judith Butler's phrase, a "gender trouble";[1] second, Faulkner's own feminism, especially that expressed in such later novels as *Requiem for a Nun*, *The Town*, and *The Mansion*, has been neglected until recently. If we want to discuss Faulkner's influence on Oe, however, we cannot dismiss the fact that Oe is one of the rare students of Faulkner's later novels, and his interest in the later novels is mainly concerned with Faulkner's representation of the feminine in those novels.

As we have seen in the previous chapter, Oe's Yoknapatawpha-like cosmology includes a criticism of Japan's Emperor-centered cosmology. In *The Silent Cry*, *Dojidai gemu*, *M/T to mori no fushigi no monogatari*, and *Natsukashii toshi e no tegami*, Oe presents his own native village as Japan's caricatured double. Since it is a double, however, while criticizing Japan, it is always in danger of ending up simply mirroring Japan. Especially, what is missing in those novels is an eye on Japan's patriarchy. As we have seen, however, *"Ame no ki" o kiku onna tachi*, published in 1982, is already an exploration into the femininity of *"is"* as expressed by Penny and opposed to the male sense of time felt by "I" and Takayasu Kacchan. Furthermore, such an opposition between the feminine and the masculine has already been suggested in the 1971 novella, "The Day He Himself Shall Wipe My Tears Away," in the form of opposition between "he"'s mother's criticism and "he"'s and his father's common belief in the Emperor's immortality. Although we can trace the origin of such an opposition between the feminine and the masculine even to *The Silent Cry*, in which Mitsu's leap is brought by his wife's criticism, we can settle the date of Oe's intensive tackling with the opposition between the feminine and the masculine in the 1980s. In that decade, as he develops his own Yoknapatawpha through *M/T to mori no fushigi no monogatari*, and *Natsukashii toshi e no tegami*, Oe at the same time engages himself in the revision of gender in his novels.

The 1981 speech on Faulkner, entitled "Reading Faulkner from a Writer's Point of View," is the earliest sign of Oe's feminist turn. Discussing the male and female characters in the Snopes trilogy, *If I Forget Thee, Jerusalem*, and *Absalom, Absalom!* Oe sees a "chasm" between them. According to Oe, such characters as Eula and Linda Snopes, or Charlotte Rittenmeyer, represent the female archetype, and such male characters as Gavin Stevens and Harry Wilbourne are the catalysts, and, most importantly, a "chasm" between them enables the author, Faulkner, to exert his imagination (73). Oe's remarks on the chasm between Faulkner's male and female characters look like just another expression of what has been frequently said about *The Sound and the Fury*, in particular, as André Bleikasten argues, Caddy's being a "primal gap," "pure figure of *absence*," "empty signifier," or a "symbolic reminder, perhaps, of the mythic mediating function of woman through whom, for man, passes all knowledge about the origin, all knowledge about the twin enigmas of life and death" (53–56). Moreover, as to Eula as the female archetype, Cleanth Brooks has already pointed out that, for the whole community of Frenchman's Bend, she "becomes the archetypal feminine" (172). Also, we can suspect that Oe might probably refer to David Williams's basically Jungian study of Faulkner, which quotes from Erich Neumann's *Great Mother*: "If we survey the whole of the symbolic sphere determined by the vessel character of the Archetypal Feminine, we find that in its elementary and transformative character the Feminine as 'creative principle' encompasses the whole world" (53).[2]

Apart from the question of originality of Oe's view, what Oe sees in the chasm between Faulkner's male and female characters forms part of his feminist turn in the 1980s. Toward the end of the 1980s, Oe wrote two of his most successful female-centered novels, that is, *Jinsei no shinseki* (*An Echo of Heaven*, 1989), which presented a female protagonist for the first time in Oe's career, and *Shizukana seikatsu* (*A Quiet Life*, 1990), which also presented for the first time a female narrator-protagonist. Along with those two novels, the 1981 speech on Faulkner, the famous two interviews with two of the leading female novelists, Tomioka Taeko and Tsushima Yuko, in 1985,[3] and the publication of *Atarashii bungaku no tameni* (For a New Literature), his second book on novelistic methodology (the first one is *Shosetsu no hoho* [1978]) in 1988, which includes the recapitulation of the 1981 speech on Faulkner, form Oe's consecutive efforts to bring about a "gender trouble" in his writings. It would not be too much to say that were it not for those efforts in the 1980s, the androgynous character-narrator in the Flaming Green Tree trilogy (1993, 1994, 1995) or the focal character's homosexuality in *Somersault* (1999) could never be conceived.[4]

We can trace a change even in Oe's treatment of Caddy-like sister figure in his own Yoknapatawpha novels. In the 1967 novel, *The Silent Cry*, Oe apparently refers to the relationship between Quentin and Caddy in *The Sound and the Fury* in characterizing Taka's relation with his mentally deficient sister. As Ikuko Fujihira points out, just as Quentin imagines being burned in hell with Caddy, Taka—to be precise, Taka according to Mitsu's imagination—tries to see in the picture of hell drawn by the great-grandfather the end of his incestuous relationship with his sister ("The Image of Hell"). Like Caddy for Quentin, Taka's sister represents the center of his ideal life as separate from the detestable reality. Taka's sister, in this sense, especially after her death, is an absent center around or toward which his, or Mitsu's, imagination works. Such a sister figure as represented by Caddy is also used in the 1979 novel, *Dojidai gemu*. In the novel, the narrator "I," who is doomed by his father to become the inheritor and transmitter of the "myth and history of their village=nation= microcosm," thinks of raping his sister, who is also doomed by his father to become the virgin to be consecrated to *Kowasuhito*, and of being driven away from the village together. For "I," this seems to be the only way out from the doom common to both himself and his sister. "I" resembles Quentin who wishes to take Caddy away to hell, where she *"will have only me then only me then the two of us amid the pointing and the horror beyond the clean flame"* (Faulkner, *The Sound and the Fury* 133).

In the 1986 novel, *M/T to mori no fushigi no monogatari*, a retelling of the story told in *Dojidai gemu*, however, Oe abandons the relationship between the male protagonist and the Caddy-like sister figure. Instead, Oe brings in his saga the narrative framework in which the female principle, (M)atriarch, and the male principle, (T)rickster, complement each other. The history of the fictional village is narrated by the same male narrator "I" as in *Dojidai gemu*, but the source of "I" is no longer his father, but his grandmother. Unlike *Dojidai gemu*, neither father nor sister occupies "I"'s mind. The story itself is no longer centered on *Kowasuhito*, the ruling male principle in *Dojidai gemu*. Instead, it is restructured as the repetition of the complementary relationship between the recurrent M and T figures, of which grandmother and "I" are a part. Moreover, in the

1987 novel, *Natsukashii toshi eno tegami*, we see as many female characters as we have ever seen in Oe's previous novels. Oe himself reveals that, in writing the novel, he thought of creating ten female types (Enomoto 259). "I"'s sister is only one of them. What runs through the whole narrative is the relationship between Dante, Virgil, and Beatrice, that is, "I" as Dante, Brother Gii as Virgil and ten female characters as Beatrice (Enomoto 259). Unlike Beatrice or a Caddy-like sister, however, those ten female characters are not the source of "I"'s imagination. Rather, they represent the ubiquitous feminine, which replaces *Kowasuhito*, the ubiquitous masculine, in *Dojidai gemu*.

In both *M/T to mori no fushigi no monogatari* and *Natsukashii toshi eno tegami*, Oe tries to shake up the autonomy of the male-centered microcosm contained in *The Silent Cry* and *Dojidai gemu* by applying the complementarity between M (the female principle) and T (the male principle) or the ubiquitous presence of Beatrice as the "female 'Other'" (Butler xxviii) on which the male subjects must always depend. Both novels are the result of the "gender trouble" on which Oe has worked since the beginning of the 1980s. The literary devices of M/T and ten female types have served to cause a tremendous change in Oe's literary cosmos. However, there still remains a crucial problem. In *M/T to mori no fushigi no monogatari* and *Natsukashii toshi eno tegami*, in spite of the increase in feminine elements here and there in both the narrative framework and the story narrated, Oe's recurrent first-person male narrator is still holding the reins of the whole narrative. In this sense, the feminine in *M/T to mori no fushigi no monogatari* and *Natsukashii toshi eno tegami*—be it Matriarch or Beatrice—is still not so different from Caddy: the feminine still provides the vessel, whereas the male "I" fills the vessel with his words.

Here we have to consider another curious fact. More than the lack of female elements, Oe's novels are generally characterized by the absence of father. This may sound incongruous, since we know that half of Oe's literary fame has come from the novels and essays in which Oe centrally depicts the relationship between father and son modeled on Oe himself and his son Hikari. In those novels concerning father and son, father is always Oe himself, not Oe's father. Even in *Pinchi ranna chosho* (*The Pinch Runner Memorandum*), in which father and son exchange places in a slapstick manner, the father figure is still based on Oe, not on his son or father. Although Oe has borrowed from Faulkner the relation between Quentin and Caddy in *The Silent Cry* and *Dojidai gemu*, Oe has never used the motif of conflictual or oedipal relationship between father and son as represented by the relationship between Quentin and his father in *The Sound and the Fury*, Henry and Thomas Sutpen in *Absalom, Absalom!*, or the corporal and the old general in *A Fable*. Of course, there are pieces in which a father of the protagonist who is a fictional equivalent to Oe himself appears; among them are included *Okurete kita seinen* (The Youth Who Came Late, 1962), *Dojidai gemu*, "Chichi yo anata wa doko e ikunoka?" (Where Are You Going, Father? 1968), and "The Day He Himself Shall Wipe My Tears Away." Even in those novels and short stories, however, the father does not doom his son as Quentin's father, Thomas Sutpen, and the old general do; he looks more like some stranger who temporarily influences a young man's thoughts.

This general absence of a father figure from Oe's works can be ascribed to the fact that Oe has lost his father at the age of nine; the relation with his father does not occupy much space in his memories of childhood. Instead, as we have seen in the previous chapter with "The Day He Himself Shall Wipe My Tears Away," it is the Emperor who plays the role of father in Oe's imagination. However, there is even a change in the Emperor figures, since the older Emperor-centered system fell when Oe was ten years old, that is, when Japan lost World War II. So, it is the Emperor as defined as symbol of Japan in the Japanese post-World War II constitution, or the Emperor as metaphor for the imagined community called postwar Japan, that emerged in Oe's imagination as father. The Emperor, in this sense, is an ultimate father figure for the Japanese postwar society, or, in other words, a metaphor for the general phallocentrism that binds the imagination of every Japanese, which Lacanians might call the Name-of-the-Father.[5] For Oe, to bring a "gender trouble" into his literary cosmos is a necessary strategy to challenge such an established symbolic or metaphorical order found in both Japanese society and in his own imagination. If, as we have seen, Oe's fictional village is to function as a strategic metaphor for Japan, it should not look like Japan's clone. Rather it should be an amalgam of caricature and criticism. For Oe, the feminine is a means to criticize Japanese society by degrading and lowering its male-oriented spiritual values. However, as far as the 1986 novel, *M/T to mori no fushigi no monogatari*, and the 1987 novel, *Natsukashii toshi e no tegami*, are concerned, Oe's "gender trouble" has not gone far enough, because both novels still rely on the key agent of Japanese male-centered ways of thinking, especially the male first-person narration. In other words, up until this point, Oe's limited ambition to cause a "gender trouble" in his critical representation of Japan is made evident by his recurrent or even habitual "I" or eye—the male first-person narrator.

An Echo of Heaven and *A Quiet Life* are the texts that mark a "gender trouble" in Oe's recurrent male first-person narration. Oe's 1981 speech on Faulkner should be read in this context. In its recapitulation included in the 1987 book, *Atarashii bungaku no tameni*, Oe focuses on the chasm between Gavin and Eula or Linda, in the context in which he explains defamilialization (Russian Formalism) and degradation and lowering (Bakhtin's grotesque realism). For Oe, the female archetype as represented by Eula and Linda is part of the literary methodology which enables one's imagination to shuttle between the "ordinary" 日常的なもの and the "mythical" 神話的なもの (*Atarashii bungaku no tameni* 146). What is implied here is the criticism of the authoritarian myth of the imperial Japan that was transmitted through school education before World War II. Oe asserts, in a somewhat abrupt manner, that "there is no creative energy in a myth as fixed as the one found in the school textbooks before and during the war" (my translation); 戦前・戦中の

教科書にあったような、固定された神話には、創造的なエネルギーは
ない (146).

Together with the female archetype, Oe refers to the study of the
child archetype by C. G. Jung and C. Kerényi. Especially, Oe summarizes Jung's description of four phenomenal characteristics of the
child archetype: that is, the abandonment of the child, the invinci-
bility of the child, the hermaphroditism of the child, and the child as
beginning and end (*Atarashii bungaku no tameni* 149–51).[6] Although
Oe does not try to elucidate the connection, it is not difficult for us to
guess why for Oe the child archetype is associated with the female
archetype. Among others, the motif of abandoned or deserted child is
especially relevant to Oe's effort to subvert the authoritarian patriarchal society as represented in his own literary cosmos. As we will
see with *A Quiet Life*, Oe tries to decenter the symbiotic relationship
between father and mentally handicapped son, which is the motif of
most of his previous novels based on the life with his family, with the
sister-daughter-narrator's obsession with the idea of her brother as
being abandoned or deserted by his father. This clearly indicates a
change in Oe's views of a Caddy-like sister figure. In *A Quiet Life*,
Oe's interest is no longer in the relationship between Quentin (the
subject) and Caddy (the object), to which he has referred in *The Silent
Cry* and *Dojidai gemu*. Rather, Oe is more interested in "Caddy's
political role in the Compson family," that is, the figure of Caddy who
"expresses a hatred for 'everything' as she cries in Maury/Benjy's
lap," and "[i]n defiance of her parents . . . continues to call the boy
Maury on occasion" (Urgo, *Faulkner's Apocrypha* 40). In other words,
for Oe, creating a sister-daughter-narrator in *A Quiet Life* is equivalent to "'hear' Caddy Compson as the feminine voice of difference
within male discourse, as the counter-narrative that speaks the possibility of play" (Gwin 27).

A Quiet Life is a novel about a female narrator-protagonist who is
troubled by the problem of suffering children. In this sense, we should
read it also in comparison with *Requiem for a Nun*, in which Temple
Drake Stevens is led by both Gavin Stevens and Nancy Mannigoe to

cope with the suffering of her own children, whom she deserted *de facto*. The focus of our comparison, however, lies not so much in the suffering of children as in the suffering of those heroines—Ma-chan in *A Quiet Life* and Temple in *Requiem for a Nun*—whose voices, or whose feminine discourses, are forced to remain silent, or invisible. In *Requiem for a Nun*, Temple struggles to describe her life, especially the motives for leaving her family, with her own words, but Stevens and Nancy always intervene and force on her their views of life.[7] Temple's difficulties in appropriating her life to herself is very much like Ma-chan's in *A Quiet Life*.

In what follows, we will see more about how Oe's feminist turn which begins in his discovery of the chasm between Faulkner's female and male characters—especially that between Eula/Linda and Gavin in *The Town* and *The Mansion*—results in *An Echo of Heaven*. We will also see how the feminine discourse of Temple in *Requiem for a Nun* resonates in Ma-chan's first-person narration in *A Quiet Life*, especially in terms of the motif of the abandoned or deserted child, and of her struggle in the subject-object relation with her father.

Distancing

The Town and *The Mansion*

In the recapitulation of the 1981 speech on Faulkner included in the 1988 book *Atarashii bungaku no tameni*, Oe repeats almost word for word what he has said in the speech concerning the chasm, or distance, between Eula/Linda the female archetype and Gavin the catalyst:

ギャヴィンは、ユーラ－リンダの両者から誘いかけら
れながら、あこがれつづけている相手と肉体的な愛を
成就することはない。かれの意識するままにいえば、
その時は私は私ではなくなってしまうからだ。そして
フォークナーという書き手の立場からいえば、それは
ユーラ－リンダという女性的元型を、想像力的にこれ

ほどよく機能させる受け手を失ってしまうことになる
からである。
　ギャヴィンにそくしていうなら、かれがユーラおよ
びリンダとの肉体的な接触を自分に禁じつづける態度
は、その想像力のうちに生きて働くユーラーリンダ像
の密度をさらに濃くし、その想像力の危機的な緊張を
さらに高める役割をはたしている。いつまでも埋めら
れない溝をなかにはさみながら、実現不可能な跳びこ
えを試みつづけること。それが想像力の働きの基本的
なしくみのひとつなのだ。(163-64)

Gavin never tries to achieve the physical relationships with
Eula and Linda, for whom he has been yearning, and both of
whom have tempted him themselves, because, as he himself
realizes, he would not have been him then. From the point
of view of Faulkner the writer, that would cost him a
character/instrument which can activate Eula and Linda as
the female archetype so lively as Gavin has done in his
imagination.

　From Gavin's point of view, his asceticism, which has
been prohibiting him from having physical relationships
with Eula and Linda, at once enriches the figure of
Eula/Linda living and working in his imagination and
heightens the critical tension of such an imagination.
While maintaining the gap which cannot be leaped, Gavin
continually tries to leap the gap in his imagination. This is
how his imagination works. (my translation)

Oe assumes that the chasm Gavin tries to keep between himself and
Eula/Linda is a narrative technique indispensable for Faulkner to
activate Eula and Linda as the female archetype in Gavin's
imagination. Eula and Linda are not the female archetype in
themselves. They function as the female archetype only through a
catalyst's, say Gavin's, imagination. Oe does not tell, however, which

is more important for Gavin between "enrich[ing] the figure of Eula/Linda living and working in his imagination" and "heighten[ing] the critical tension of such an imagination." Gavin wishes to come closer to Eula and Linda, but at the same time he tries to keep the distance. In *An Echo of Heaven*, Oe still uses his habitual male first-person narration. What Oe attempts in the novel, however, is to apply Gavin's chasm or distance to his male first-person narrator. In the novel, "I," the male first-person narrator, narrates the life story of Marie, the female protagonist. As he narrates her story, "I" tries to keep his distance, or the "critical tension," between himself and his subject (object), and by so doing, just like Gavin, tries rather desperately to hold on to his subjectivity.

Let us see first in *The Town* and *The Mansion* how such a distance works. *The Town* is divided into twenty four chapters and narrated by three male character-narrators—that is, Gavin, V. K. Ratliff, and Charles Mallison. We know that this is the structure of *The Sound and the Fury*, in which three Compson brothers are vouchsafed each chapter, and Caddy is placed at the center of those three men's gazes. Eula and Linda, in this sense, resemble another Caddy. Also in *The Mansion*, the chapter entitled "Linda" is subdivided into six sections, and each section is ascribed again to Gavin, Ratliff, or Mallison. The chapter "Linda" is the only chapter in *The Mansion* that is narrated this way. The other two chapters, "Mink" and "Flem," are narrated by the third-person narrator. We can here suspect Faulkner's gender-conscious intention to repeat the structure of *The Sound and the Fury* in which the central female figure is always surrounded by three male narrators. The female figure is supposed to be the object (subject) of the male observation and imagination.

Among those three male narrators, Gavin alone is personally involved with Eula and Linda. Throughout, Gavin tries, or, at least, wants, to save or separate Eula and Linda from Flem's influence. Curiously, however, Gavin never actually tries to do so. Manfred de Spain, mayor of Jefferson and Gavin's rival, actually tries to elope with Eula, though he fails because of Eula's suicide. Gavin does not

even try to touch Eula when she offers herself. Gavin tells her that
"All three gentlemen but only two were men" (*The Town* 95). "Three
gentlemen" mean Hoake McCarron (Linda's true father), Manfred,
and himself, and the "only two" mean the first two. In *The Mansion*,
Gavin does the same to Linda, who is also self-consciously repeating
what her mother has already done to Gavin. To Gavin, who says
(writes on the tablet) that he did not accept Eula's offer "*Because she
felt sorry for me when you do things for people just because you feel
sorry for them what you do is probably not very important to you,*"
Linda even tries to offer a positive reason why he has to accept her: "I
dont feel sorry for you. You know that. Dont you know it will be
important to me?" (*The Mansion* 241) Instead of accepting her offer,
Gavin writes down another explanation why he did not accept her
mother's offer, though he rips the paper off and simply rewrites: "*I
must go now.*" In the ripped paper, Gavin writes: "*Then maybe it was
because I wasnt worthy of her & we both knew it but I thought if we
didnt maybe she might always think maybe I might have been*" (241).
Eula has already described such a self-complacent way of Gavin's
guessing as "spend[ing] too much time expecting" or "wast[ing] time
expecting" (*The Town* 94). In *The Mansion*, Linda repeats almost the
same description as she proposes Gavin to marry Melisandre Backus
so that she and he can be on equal terms: "Do you remember back
there at the beach when the sun finally went down and there was
nothing except the sunset and the pines and the sand and the ocean
and you and me and I said how that shouldn't be wasted after all that
waiting and distance" (250–51). Here, Linda even cooperates with
Gavin in keeping the distance between them. In *The Town*, Gavin has
already asked Linda if she wants to marry him, and Linda has
answered yes. But by asking again, Gavin implicitly takes his
proposal back, and makes Linda say, "I dont want to marry anybody!"
(*The Town* 193) In *The Mansion*, Gavin's promise to marry
Melisandre Backus is another means to keep the distance, and to keep
thinking of Linda. The wall between two rooms in the hotel at
Pascagoula realizes such a mental distance.

For Gavin, the distance between himself and Eula/Linda functions as the bulwark to protect his subjectivity. In other words, Gavin's subjectivity is expressed not as what he expects, but rather as the distance he keeps to what he is expecting. Therefore, when Eula advises, "Dont expect. You just are, and you need, and you must, and so you do," she is threatening Gavin's subjectivity (*The Town* 94).[8] Against her advice, as Oe says, Gavin desperately tries to keep the distance, by saying, "If I had just had sense enough to say *I am, I want, I will and so here goes*—If I had just done that, . . . I wouldn't have been me then?" In who or what Gavin is, however, Eula shows no interest: "she wasn't even listening: just looking at me: the unbearable and unfathomable blue, speculative and serene." Eula is not simply indifferent to Gavin's sense of what he is; she has already seen through Gavin's habit of distancing, or romanticizing. With his romantic bent, Gavin likens Eula, or her threat to his subjectivity, to the "sea" or an "envelopment" (92, 93, 95).[9] Eula calls people like Gavin, not Gavin alone, or not men alone, "unhappy": "I dont like unhappy people. They are a nuisance" (93). As we have seen in the previous chapter, Gavin mistakes those words by Eula for an expression of "compassion" and "pity" for him. But Eula is not talking about Gavin alone. Eula is thinking of all men who surround her, and, more or less, of herself, too. Eula can see through Gavin's distancing, because she sees something similar in herself too. In the previous chapter, we have already assumed Eula's motive to come to Gavin's office to be concerned with "AWARE." Eula's "AWARE" is not simply a compassion or pity for Gavin but an understanding of the general condition in which a modern person's life is caught, or the fundamental awareness of being alienated from what she calls "You just are, and you need, and you must, and so you do," which represents a sense of time that does not separate now from then, or knows no boundary between subject and object. In other words, Eula is paraphrasing what Faulkner calls "*is*." When Eula tells Gavin not to expect, therefore, she is not so much urging Gavin to take her as criticizing him for trying to stop the motion of "You just are, and you need, and you must, and so you do." Eula herself is also lost to "*is*." Telling Gavin "you just are," she is trying to understand or recall what "*is*" is, even if she knows she can never realize it. Gavin does not understand what Eula means. His habitual distancing, waiting, expecting, romanticism, sense of himself, or sense of subjectivity, hinders him from understanding Eula's "AWARE" or Faulkner's "*is*."

After the second visit to Gavin's office narrated in Chapter 20, Eula kills herself. Ratliff says, "she was bored" (*The Town* 358). Gavin agrees and thinks that Eula could not find anybody who matched her "capacity to love," "to find somebody not just strong enough to deserve, earn it, match it, but even brave enough to accept it" (359). If by "capacity to love" Gavin meant her "AWARE" or sense of "*is*" in Eula, he might be right. But he does not seem to mean it. On the contrary, he seems to be still thinking of himself, or his having failed to be the one who matches Eula's "capacity to love." Gavin assumes that Eula killed herself because she could not find a man who could fulfill her "capacity to love." The truth, however, is that Eula killed herself because she knew that she herself could not behave like "You just are, and you need, and you must, and so you do." In other words, Eula killed herself because she could not stand the grief which accompanied her own sense of "*is*." As we have seen with Oe's "'Ame no ki' o kiku onnatachi," "AWARE" or "*is*," which is associated in Oe's short story with the "rain tree" and grief, represents a repressed sense of time that might suddenly erupt in a modern person's psyche, and cause a wish to escape from everyday life, to go home, to the womb, or to death. Eula is a kind of person who holds such a wish for a long time.

Although the text does not tell us exactly when Eula decides to kill herself (Eula's suicide seems rather abrupt), when Eula says to Gavin in their first meeting fourteen years prior to her suicide, "You just are, and you need, and you must, and so you do," she has already expressed her fundamental wish to go home (in a metaphorical sense). As to the means to do so, she is not yet certain. It can be elopement, suicide, or other. In their second meeting two years prior to her suicide, Eula says to Gavin, "Women aren't interested in poets' dreams. They are interested in facts. It doesn't even matter whether the facts are true or not, as long as they match the other facts without leaving a rough seam" (*The Town* 226). In the last meeting, Eula also says, "maybe men are just interested in facts too and the only difference is, women dont care whether they are facts or not just so they fit, and men dont care whether they fit or not just so they are facts" (330-31). Taking Eula at her words, Cleanth Brooks assumes that Eula killed herself to make facts look fit, that is, to set off the fact of her suicide against her adultery.[10] However, Eula does not yet seem to be interested in killing herself at this point. "Facts" in Eula's words mean but one thing: Gavin's promise to marry Linda. Linda is the only concern for Eula, who none the less has to leave her daughter for her most selfish yet irresistible inner reason. By saying that women are interested in facts, Eula is simply trying to persuade Gavin to marry and take care of her daughter after her elopement. In her last meeting with Gavin, Eula still suggests an elopement with Manfred. Perhaps, Eula's decision to kill herself is a last-second decision, or what Oe would call leap, which we have seen in the previous chapter. After leaving Gavin's office for the last time, Eula's inner reason finally finds its outward expression in suicide. Then, we should say that Eula killed herself for no practical reason.

It is Eula, not Gavin, who understands what "*is*" is. After the last meeting with Eula, Gavin thinks: "And then I heard the door and it was as if she had not been. No, not that; not *not been*, but rather no more *is*, since *was* remains always and forever, inexplicable and immune, which is its grief" (Faulkner, *The Town* 334). Here we can hear the echo of what Faulkner said in the Jean Stein interview: "There is no such thing as *was*—only *is*. If *was* existed there would be no grief or sorrow" (255). Curiously, however, we can see here a change, or even a reversal, in the relationship between "*is*" and "*was*." In the Jean Stein interview, which was held exactly when Faulkner was writing *The Town*, "*is*" exists, while "*was*" does not; on the other hand, for Gavin in *The Town*, there is "*no more is*," while "*was*" remains forever. Of course, we can dismiss this change as another Faulkner inconsistency. Or, we can interpret both as meaning eventually the same: whether he calls it "*is*" or "*was*," what is important for Faulkner is the idea of time that is in a "fluid condition," and Gavin's idea of time that "remains" is merely another expression. However, there is a crucial evidence that tells us that Gavin is confusing Faulkner's "*is*" and "*was*." Gavin's theory of "*was*"—"'*was*' remains, as if what is going to happen to one tomorrow already gleams faintly visible now if the watcher were only wise enough to discern it or maybe just brave enough"—is soon undermined by the fact that he could not foretell Eula's suicide. Or, on the contrary, it might be more appropriate to say that Gavin's "*was*" successfully and uncannily foretold Eula's becoming eternal "*was*." Gavin swears to marry Linda, and sees Eula off, watching her "los[e] dimension now, onto or rather into the shadow of the little gallery and losing substance now" (Faulkner, *The Town* 334). Gavin seems to be glad to see Eula leaving, to see Eula off into the image of "*was*," a static image that reminds us of the images on Keats' Grecian urn. In the Jean Stein interview, Faulkner also speaks for Gavin, who is an artist or a poet for whom "the *Ode on a Grecian Urn* is worth any number of old ladies" (239), or whose aim is "to arrest motion, which is life, by artificial means and hold it fixed so that 100 years later when a stranger looks at it, it moves again since it is life" (253). For Gavin, however, "*was*," not "*is*," is the aim of his art. "*Was*" for Gavin is also the means to fix Eula in the past, or to see her off into the future that he can predict. What Gavin expects to appear in the future is the same image of Eula as he saw it today, that is, the image he calls "*was*." Fixing Eula as "*was*" enables Gavin to keep the distance from her. In this sense, "grief," which Gavin associates with the image of "*was*," is nothing but another expression of the distance he wants to keep, or his sense of subjectivity that he can consolidate only by keeping the distance from what he wants.

Gavin keeps seeing Eula from a distance, and keeps her in his imagination as a female archetype. That is the way he protects his subjectivity. However, Gavin's subjectivity has already been severely challenged, if only he would accede to it. Eula's own words have already revealed her inner life as she lives it, and her "AWARE" or sense of "*is*" has overwhelmed Gavin's "*was*." In their last meeting, after listening to Eula explain how she has been driven to the situation, which allows her no way out but to elope with Manfred, Gavin suggests rather stupidly that, at least, Eula no longer has to sleep with Flem. "Oh, that," Eula says, and continues:

> You mean that. That doesn't matter. That's never been any trouble. He . . . cant. He's—what's the word?—impotent. He's always been. Maybe that's why, one of the reasons. You see? You've got to be careful or you'll have to pity him. You'll have to. He couldn't bear that, and it's no use to hurt people if you dont get anything for it. (*The Town* 331)

Eula reveals Flem's impotence. In doing so, Eula equates Gavin's distancing, or even his subjectivity, with her husband's impotence: that is, Gavin is not physically impotent, but he is mentally, or romantically, impotent. Eula warns Gavin not to pity Flem, since pitying Flem means for Gavin to pity himself. Curiously enough, however, Gavin has already anticipated all this in the first meeting with Eula, in which he equates Manfred, his rival, with Hoake McCarron, Linda's father, and calls them "men" (95), and at the same time, realizes for the first time that Flem is impotent. Gavin thinks both Manfred and Hoake McCarron alike, and that leaves both Flem and himself also alike, that is, impotent. Nevertheless, at this point, Gavin is not yet so sure about Flem's actual impotence. That is why, in their last meeting, he can still ask Eula about the nights with Flem. Flem is Gavin's enemy, and, as a man who actually got Eula for his wife, another means for Gavin to clarify his difference, his identity as one who keeps a distance from Eula. For Gavin, pity can be a threat to his identity, because pity makes him and Flem look alike. Gavin has to try not to understand the pity that Eula suspects between him and her husband.

In Eula's revelation of her husband's impotence, however, there is another yet more important message that Gavin does not understand. By warning Gavin not to pity Flem, Eula also asks him not to pity her, since Eula knows that she is also impotent in the sense that she has not matched up to what she calls "You just are, and you need, and you must, and so you do." What Eula means by pity here is an "AWARE," or a sense of "*is*," or, to be more precise, a sense of being alienated from "*is*." By warning Gavin not to pity Flem, therefore, Eula is pointing out the common fate which has engulfed Flem, Gavin, and herself, and by so doing, she has already been pitying all three of them. Eula sees the general human condition in terms of "*is*," whereas Gavin sees Eula in his image of "*was*" and is satisfied with it. Gavin does not realize that Eula, whom he regards as the "sea" or "envelopment," has already engulfed his subjectivity and merged it with the others. Finally, Eula's abrupt suicide leaves every man of Jefferson—including Manfred, with whom she was supposed to catch up with her "*is*"—behind, and makes all men, or even all people, alike.[11]

After Eula's suicide, Linda is even more powerful in engulfing Gavin's subjectivity. Linda is a special attraction for feminist critics: Linda is "that rare thing in Faulkner: a *political* person" (Roberts, "Eula, Linda, and the Death of Nature" 167), or a "freak, an anomaly" (170); "Linda is a 'speaking' woman too profoundly injured to be heard by anyone but Gavin" (Crabtree 538); Linda is "'(her own) writing,' the arrival of a new feminine discourse" (Kang 28). Linda marries Barton Kohl, sculptor and communist, fights for the Loyalists in the Spanish Civil War, comes back to Jefferson after losing her husband and eardrums, and works for the education of the black children, not minding being labeled "*Nigger Lover*" (Faulkner, *The Mansion* 226). In a sense, this is due to Gavin's education, his efforts of "forming her mind" (*The Town* 179), but Linda far exceeds Gavin's plan, in which he, as a teacher, at the same time keeps a safe distance from her and possesses her spiritually. Even Linda's deafness threatens Gavin's peace and the safe distance. Linda's daringness in offering herself shocks Gavin: "'But you can [blank] me,' she said. That's right. She used the explicit word, speaking the hard brutal guttural in the quacking duck's voice" (*The Mansion* 238). Linda has the power which, more than her mother's, attracts people around her into her orbit. Ratliff sees that through when he and Gavin go to New York to meet Linda, her husband, and her father Hoake McCarron:

> it was that gal that done it—that gal that never had seen one of us and fur as I actively heard it to take a oath, never had said much more than good morning to the other two—that gal that likely not even knowed but didn't even care that she had inherited her maw's fatality to draw four men anyhow to that web, that one strangling hair. (*The Mansion* 170)

Apart from his habit of mystification, or his own—like Gavin's—taste for literature as represented in his view of Linda as "fatality," that is, femme fatale, Ratliff is right in pointing out Linda's presence as a prompter of the relativity of male subjectivity. In fact, in *The Mansion*, the chapter "Linda" is placed between two other chapters "Mink" and "Flem." Linda is not a minor episode inserted into the whole revenge play enacted between Mink and Flem. Although James Gray Watson writes that "[w]ith her return to Jefferson, then, Linda becomes part of the recurrent pattern of isolation and revenge established in the section of *The Mansion* that is devoted to Mink" (180), it is Linda who changes the pattern of frustration and failure established by Mink, and directs the whole narrative of *The Mansion* to revenge and the destruction of the authoritarian male subjectivity, which is represented by Flem, her father.[12]

Linda signs a petition to help Mink out of jail, and as soon as she knows that Mink can get the pardon, she orders a Jaguar so that she can leave Jefferson after her father's death. Indirectly, yet *de facto*, Linda kills Flem. But what hurts Gavin most is the fact that Linda purposely let him know her will to kill her father by "let[ting] him discover the new Jaguar and what it implied in the circumstances of her so-called father's death," and forces an understanding between him and her that "she knew he knew it" (*The Mansion* 425). Gavin now calls such a mutual understanding, or even love, "their curse." By turning a love into a curse, Linda has abused the description of their relationship, which they shared in the night at Pascagoula, as "two people in all the earth out of all the world that can love each other not only without having to but we dont even have to not say that word you dont like to hear" (*The Mansion* 252). Linda does not "have to not say that word," so she says it. That is, by letting Gavin discover her Jaguar, Linda implicitly says that she has already killed Flem, her father. Whether he likes it or not, Gavin has already been involved in patricide.

However, there is more in Linda's implicit message to Gavin. Linda knows that Gavin is like another father to her, or has been even trying to take Flem's place through "forming her mind." By letting Gavin know that she has killed Flem, Linda also declares that she has killed Gavin in her. This is the crux of Linda's murder of Flem: it is not so much Flem as Gavin whom Linda killed. To understand this, we have to go back to Chapter Eight of *The Town*, in which Linda appears for the first time in the world of Gavin's imagination and Gavin imagines himself as her father or grandfather:

> So that girl-child was not Flem Snopes's at all, but mine; my child and my grandchild both, since the McCarron boy who begot her (oh yes, I can even believe Ratliff when it suits me) in that lost time, was Gavin Stevens in that lost time; and, since remaining must remain or quit being remaining, Gavin Stevens is fixed by his own child forever at that one age in that one moment. So since the son is father to the man, the McCarron fixed forever and timeless in that dead youth as Gavin Stevens is of necessity now the son of Gavin Stevens's age, and McCarron's child is Gavin

Stevens's grandchild. (*The Town* 135–36).

We can see here another example in which Gavin confuses "*is*" and
"*was*." Although Gavin criticizes a poet who sings, "That Fancy
passed me by And nothing will remain," and insists that "it is
Remaining which will always remain," Gavin is another poet who
prefers "Motion" as fixed in "*was*" (Gavin says, "I also am Motion")
to motion as "*is*" (135). In his imagination, Gavin equates himself
with McCarron who begot Linda "in that lost time." Gavin thinks that
as soon as he (Gavin-McCarron) begot the child he was fixed at that
age and privileged to remain forever. What is fixed and remains is the
father and what fixes the father is the son; in this sense, the son is the
father to, or the creator of, the man. If McCarron is Linda's father
because he was fixed directly by Linda's birth, Gavin is her grandfather because he was also, yet indirectly, or imaginatively, fixed by
her birth.

But why father and son? Gavin's idea of "Remaining" is linked to
the idea of patriarchal succession. In Gavin's "Remaining," what is
fixed and remains is each patriarch. Gavin finds the illustration of
such a "Remaining" in the Snopes clan:

> So this was not the first time I ever thought how apparently
> all Snopeses are male, as if the mere and simple incident
> of woman's divinity precluded Snopesishness and made it
> paradox. No: it was rather as if *Snopes* were some pro-
> found and incontrovertible hermaphroditic principle for
> the furtherance of a race, a species, the principle vested
> always physically in the male, any anonymous conceptive
> or gestative organ drawn into that radius to conceive and
> spawn, repeating that male principle and then vanishing.
> (*The Town* 136)

Snopesism is not Gavin's enemy. Rather, it represents the general
male principle to which Gavin also belongs. By imagining himself as

father or grandfather of Linda, Gavin expresses his desire to be a
chief component of such a male principle. Gavin also calls the male
principle "Motion." In Gavin's patriarchal imagination, Eula and
Linda are nothing but "a part of," or a "mortality" that is "doomed to
fade" in, the Motion created by the male desire which alone per-
petuates (*The Town* 132–33).

What Gavin calls "Remaining," "*was*," or "Motion" is different
from what Faulkner calls "*is*." Gavin's "Remaining," "*was*," or "Motion" signifies the male principle as represented by the Snopes clan,
whereas Faulkner's "*is*," as expressed by Eula rather than Gavin, is
the more general condition which applies to both male and female.
Gavin sounds as if he is foretelling Eula's suicide. But Eula's suicide
is not, as Gavin sees it, an "act of quitting Motion," the male principle; rather, Eula's suicide is an act of quitting the condition in which
she is alienated from what she calls "You just are, and you need, and
you must, and so you do." In a sense, it may be true that Eula's
suicide is an act of quitting "Motion," since "Motion," the male
principle, can be the cause of Eula's sense of alienation from "You
just are, and you need, and you must, and so you do." At least, Linda
thinks so. Otherwise, Linda does not have to purposely let Gavin
know her will to kill her father, or involve Gavin in her revenge.
Knowing that Gavin imaginatively identifies himself with the Snopes
male principle, Linda also imaginatively kills him. If Gavin's subjectivity is based on the distance which he keeps between his "*was*"
and her mother's, and her own, sense of "*is*," Linda has to let him
know that such a subjectivity is a patriarchal illusion.

After killing the Father, Linda leaves Jefferson. Ironically, it is
Gavin who has urged Linda to leave Jefferson so that she can be
liberated from her father's, that is, Flem's influence. Now Linda
leaves the Father, which both Flem and Gavin represent. We can hear
in such a figure of Linda an echo of the ending of *Flags in the Dust*,
in which a female consciousness that belongs to both Miss Jenny and
Narcissa thinks: "perhaps Sartoris is the name of the game itself—a
game outmoded and played with pawns shaped too late and to an old

dead pattern, and of which the Player Himself is a little wearied"
(433). Sartoris here can be replaced by Snopes.

What we see in *The Town* and *The Mansion*, therefore, is Faulkner's feminist attack on patriarchy, or his ongoing efforts to keep the
world in motion by subverting the male principle of fixing or
objectifying the world from the standpoint of the subject. When Oe
speaks of the distance between Gavin and Eula/Linda, he seems, at
least, to have already headed for a similar subversive feminism of his
own. It is true that the speech itself, in which Oe's sympathy remains
always with Gavin, seems to be totally inattentive to Eula's fundamental discontent with, or even Linda's hostility toward, Gavin. In
this sense, it is basically male-oriented. However, in his 1989 novel
An Echo of Heaven, which clearly draws on the motif of the distance
between the male and female characters that was pointed out in the
speech, Oe, whether he intended it or not when he made the speech,
lets his female protagonist challenge the male authority, and thereby
has already outsmarted his own male authorship. As far as his novel is
concerned, then, we can apply to Oe what Gwin points out about
Faulkner: "Faulkner the author disperses himself into the writing,
dissolving into the spaces of his narrative which are sometimes
marked by woman" (123).

An Echo of Heaven

In *Jinsei no shinseki*, or *An Echo of Heaven*, Oe makes his
narrator "I" decline Marie's offer to sleep with her, and, just like
Faulkner's Gavin, try to keep the distance between himself and the
subject (object) of his narrative:

　　　──今後もう私には、あなたと一緒に夜をすごすこと
　　　はないのじゃないかしら？それならば、元気をだして
　　　一度ヤリますか？光さんが眠ってから、しのんで来ま
　　　せんか？
　　　──・・・ずっと若い頃に、かなり直接的に誘われな
　　　がらヤラなかったことが、二、三人についてあったん

だね。後からずっと悔んだものだから、ある時から、
ともかくヤルということにした時期があったけれど
も・・・いまはヤッテも・ヤラなくても、それぞれに
懐かしさがあって、ふたつはそうたいしたちがいじゃ
ないと、回想する年齢だね。
——つまりヤラなくていいわけね。・・・私も今夜のこ
とを、懐かしく思い出すと思うわ、ヤッテも、ヤラな
くても、とまり恵さんはむしろホッとした様子を示し
ていった。(174)

"I don't suppose I'll ever spend another night on my own
with you. So shall we cheer ourselves up and 'do it,' just
this once? You could sneak back here, after Hikari goes to
sleep?"

". . . When I was much younger, there were two or three
women I didn't 'do it' with, even though they propositioned
me directly. I regretted it for a long time afterward, so then I
went through a period when I decided I'd 'do it,' no matter
what. . . . But now that I'm older, I look back and realize
that whether I 'did it' or not, the memories are there all the
same, so it didn't really make much difference."

"In other words, we don't really need to 'do it.' . . .
Either way, I'm sure I'll have nice memories of tonight,"
she replied, looking more relieved than anything. (139)[13]

Although Marie agrees with "I" on the nostalgia that they will feel in
the future, there is a fundamental difference in their understandings of
how this night should be remembered. On the one hand, by fore-
stalling the nostalgia with which he will look back at the present, "I,"
like Gavin, tries to send Marie into the past (or future) and fix her as
"*was*"; on the other hand, for Marie, who has decided, after a
temporary escape with her American lover Uncle Sam, to return to the
life of spiritual struggle as a member of the Center, the night with
"I" should be another harbor. It will represent something like what

William James calls the resting place in the stream of consciousness, at which she only temporarily stops by in the current of her continuous hardship. If nostalgia for "I" means to view Marie from a distance, it means for Marie to involve "I" in the same flow of life as she herself is involved in. For Marie, therefore, whether to have sex with "I" or not is no more important than it is for Eula to have sex with Gavin. Just as Gavin is one of those "unhappy people" for Eula, "I" is nothing but another Uncle Sam for Marie.

Since the double suicide of her two sons, Marie has been holding a fundamental doubt about the righteousness of the universe. For Marie, who is a scholar of Flannery O'Connor, the death of her two sons has become a medium through which she explores the possibility of glimpsing an order (the mystery) that might exist beyond the phenomenon (the manners) of this world. At least, Marie tells "I" so. A novelist and a bookish person himself, "I" has been reading O'Connor to understand Marie, and now, listening to Marie refer to O'Connor in explaining her mental situation, "I" believes that he understands what Marie means:

> まり恵さんが秘儀（ミステリー）という言葉でいいたかったことの、
> 漠然たる輪郭は、メキシコで彼女の奇態な夢を見た後
> しばらくたって、再読し・また初めて読みもした、オ
> コナーのいくつかの評論から、推測することができた。
> 彼女の『秘儀（ミステリー）と習俗（マナーズ）』という評論集は、他のメキシコ
> で買ったほとんどの本ともども、その時点では太平洋
> を越えて送られて来つつあり、仕事場に上ってすぐ確
> かめるわけにゆかなかったが・・・それでも人間の具
> 体的な習俗を描くことをつうじて、小説が超越的なも
> ののヴィジョンをあらわす瞬間がある、という考え方
> は、自分にもよく受けとめられている、と感じたのだ。
> (93–94)

I had a vague understanding of what Marie meant by the word "mystery" from O'Connor's critical essays which I'd

reread, or seen for the first time, after that bizarre dream
in Mexico. But my copy of *Mystery and Manners*, along
with most of the books I'd bought in Mexico, was on its
way across the Pacific at the time, making it impossible to
go up to my study and check it right away. . . . Even so, her
concept of the novel, as a concrete description of manners through which moments of a transcendent vision
are revealed, was one I felt I had grasped clearly enough.
(76–77)

Although "I" pretends to speak for Marie, we have to be careful not to
believe in "I" as Marie's spokesman, nor to equate "I" with Oe. This
is a novel entitled *Jinsei no Shinseki* (*An Echo of Heaven*) written by
Oe, in which the novelist "I" narrates the story of Marie. From the
beginning, "I" has his personal reason to be concerned with Marie,
because they are both a parent to a handicapped son. But this similarity is a kind of trap for readers to be made to believe in the "I"'s
credibility as narrator-novelist. "I" tells us that he understands what
Marie means by "mystery," since he has read O'Connor. "I" also
reads Bely's *The Silent Dove* and Balzac's *Le Curé de village* and
says that Marie can be compared with those heroines. For "I," Marie
becomes more and more imaginary, and "I" even acknowledges that,
when Marie and "I"'s wife criticize him for his easy comparison
between Marie's situation and Balzac's heroine's:

　　——まず罪をおかすということがあって、その贖いが
　　ヴェロニックの生活の目標になったのなら・・・まり
　　恵さんに起った不幸と、罪をおかすということとは、
　　まったくちがうはずじゃないの？
　　　まり恵さんの気持をおもんぱかってということだろ
　　う、もとより自分の正直な感想もあわせて、妻が問い
　　かけて来た。まり恵さんも挑みかかる具合に、こうい
　　ったのだ。
　　——むしろ私のアレとヴェロニックの天然痘とを、大

きい災難として、対比しているのじゃない？というこ
とは、ヴェロニックが殺人と関係のある密通をしたよ
うに、私がこれから罪をおかすはずだと、あらかじめ
見当をつけているの？
　僕としては、手ごわいふたりの反撃にさらされてい
たわけだ。(98)

"So in Véronique's case the sin came first, and she
devoted her whole life to atoning for it. . . . But surely what
happened to Marie has got nothing to do with committing a
sin—can't you see that?" my wife protested, a desire to
defend her friend reinforcing her own natural reaction.
Marie took up the challenge where she left off.

"No, I think he meant to draw a parallel between the two
catastrophes, my loss and Véronique's smallpox. So you've
got it all figured out, have you, K? You think I'm going to
commit a mortal sin sometime soon, adultery perhaps, with
a murder lurking in the background, is that it?"

I sat there in silence, unable to defend myself against
these two formidable women. (80)

Once we recognize Oe's self-consciousness in his presenting "I" as a
self-complacent male novelist who dares to construct a narrative
about a woman, we can begin suspecting "I"'s every reference to
criticisms directed to him, including his self-criticism, as fake, or his
gesture of playing up to female or feminist audience. That is, in
reporting how he has been criticized by his wife and Marie, "I," just
like Oe himself, is feigning a self-consciousness of a novelist who has
been too much absorbed in his own imagination and the books he
reads.

Nevertheless, "I" never gives up imagining Marie in relation to
Balzac. When Asao and the other two young men who follow
Marie—those three young men remind us of Faulkner's recurrent trio
of male narrators (Benjy, Quentin, Jason, or Gavin, Ratliff, Mallison)

who surround the central female figure (Caddy or Eula/Linda)—
visit "I," "I" resumes the comparison between Marie and Balzac's
Véronique. Curiously, "I"'s wife helps "I" to resume the comparison.
When asked by those three young men how they can help Marie to
rebuild her life, and also how they should proceed with the scenario
that they are writing based on Marie's life, "I" cannot answer, and, as
a professional writer and their senior, feels embarrassed. Oe vividly
depicts the scene in which "I"'s wife tries, though reluctantly, to save
"I" from losing his face, or damaging his authority as patriarch, in
front of his own wife:

> その後の沈黙へ、脇で聞いていた妻が口を出したのだ。
> ——まり恵さんにバルザックの小説を貸したでしょ
> う？自分はムーサンと道夫くんに起ったことと関係づ
> けて読んだ、といって。朝雄さんたちにも話をしてお
> くほうがいいのじゃない？あの小説にヒントを得て、
> まり恵さんが新しいことを始めるかも知れないか
> ら・・・その時、朝雄さんたちに、受けとめる準備が
> できている方がいいはずでしょう？
> そのように妻がいう気持の底には、『村の司祭』をま
> り恵さんにすすめた時、まり恵さんにふりかかった辛
> い事故と、ヴェロニックの犯した罪から来るものとは
> ちがうといった、その抗議の思いがくすぶっていたは
> ずだ。(103)

My wife, who had been listening quietly, broke the silence.

"Remember that Balzac novel you lent Marie? She
told me she'd seen a connection with what happened to
Musan and Michio while she was reading it. Don't you
think you should tell them about it? Marie might take a hint
from the story, and start in on something new. . . . And
when that happens, they'd better be ready for it, don't you
think?"

> I could hear the lingering resentment that lay behind my
> wife's words; her angry protest when I first recommended
> *Le Curé de village* to Marie, that her friend's tragedy had no
> relation to what Véronique's sin had brought about. (84)

Oe's subversive intent is clear: "I" is a prejudiced male narrator who keeps failing to understand his female object (subject). In spite of his understanding of his wife's implicit criticism, "I" keeps telling the three young men, even all the more pleasantly, about Marie's resemblance to Véronique and his own idea of the possible scenario focusing on the "process of healing of [Marie's] soul" (85). It is even comical that "I" and three young men imagine Marie seeking to heal her soul through a "topographical reform for farmland" (87) as they learn it in Balzac.

Although the novel, as well as many other recent novels by Oe, is generally regarded as a pursuit of healing the soul, it is rather a criticism of such a male idea of healing the soul, which means nothing but a temporary fulfillment of or liberation from male sexual desire.[14] While it is true that Marie is seeking a kind of religious solution to her personal suffering, what "I"'s narrative offers her is a religious struggle under the guidance of religious leaders who are all male. Instead of engaging in a "topographical reform for farmland," instigated by those three young followers, Marie begins to work for the Japan tour of *Uchu no ishi* (the Cosmic Will), the Filipino theatrical company, led by a man nicknamed Coz, which is short for the cosmic will. This is the beginning of a series of Marie's religious ordeals, or, in other words, a series of narrative devices through which "I" turns Marie's life into one consistent, sentimentally embellished religious narrative. Throughout, Marie herself is irresolute about becoming religious, or to be more precise, acquiring a faith. For Marie, becoming religious means to regard her sons' double suicide as manifestation of some supernatural force, or, to use the terms which Marie and "I" borrow from O'Connor, to see the "mystery" in the "manners," or to make the "sensible" the "intelligible." As she herself says in her letter to "I" and his wife, however, Marie is consistent in refusing to see the "mystery" in the death of her two sons, or to think it as "intelligible": *"Needless to say, I told him I personally cant believe in tales of 'mystery' like this. I'll never be able to see what happened to Musan and Michio as 'intelligible'"* (167); あらためていうまでもなく、私自身には、こういう mystery の物語が信じられません。どうしてもムーサン、道夫くんのアレを、intelligible だとはいうことができない (211).

Marie undergoes three temptations through three male religious thinkers. After Coz, who shocks Marie by including in his performance an episode in which two brothers who resemble Marie's sons are led by some supernatural force, that is, the cosmic will, and commit double suicide, Marie is influenced by Little Father, the leader of the Center, who insists on the incarnation of Jesus Christ as the evidence of the "intelligible" that becomes the "sensible." After Little Father's death, Marie is invited by Sergio Matsuno to his community in Mexico, and asked to play the role of the Mother, a symbol of the spiritual unity of the community. Marie decides to join the community, although she does not necessarily like the idea of playing the living Virgin Mary in the community. In her letter to "I" and his wife, Marie writes about a repellent feeling that she held when Matsuno suggested a mystery, or an intervention of God, in her two sons' suicide:

私はキョトンとしていました。暗いことも暗いし、通路の石床がボートの底のように磨りへっていて、ゆっくりとしか進めぬまま、私はまだ側廊なかばにいて、脇にはあのいかにもメキシコ的なガダルーペの聖母像がかかっていました。それは混血らしい伏し目の顔ながら、チラリとこちらを見るようでもありました。私はそのままワッと泣きながら跪きそうになり、——なにくそ、なにくそ！と自分を励まして持ちこたえ、船板みたいに雨風にさらされた扉を押し開けたのです。

(213–14)

I was in a daze. It was dark inside the church, and the stone floor was so worn it curved like the bottom of a boat, which made it hard to walk on, so I was only some way down the aisle when I looked over and saw a very Mexican-looking portrait of the Virgin of Guadalupe hanging on the wall. She had her eyes cast down, as mestizo women often do, but I felt she was glancing at me. On the verge of bursting into tears and falling on my knees, I somehow got hold of myself and, taking courage, silently repeated: "NO! I WON'T! I WON'T!" as I headed for the door, made from wood as weatherbeaten as an old ship's timber, and pushed it open. (169–70)

Here, at least, "I" is not quoting Marie's letter as she wrote it; rather, "I" is paraphrasing what Marie wrote in order to assimilate it in his own sentences.[15] It is probably true that in her letter Marie denies the work of mystery in her life as well as its rendering in religious narrative. Marie says, "But when I presented what had happened in my own life in a novelistic form, the 'mystery' simply didn't appear" (167); 私の身の上に起った不幸は、小説のようにして全体を提示しても、どんな mystery にも結びついてはゆかなかったのです (210). But for "I" who is paraphrasing Marie, such a denial serves merely as a momentum for her final conversion, that is, the climax of "I"'s own religious narrative. While Marie repels Matsuno's associating her with Virgin Mary, "I" quotes the passage in which Marie expresses such a repellent feeling only to express his sympathy with Matsuno, not Marie. After quoting the letter, "I" seems to be influenced by Matsuno, not Marie. Marie's own repellent feeling to the contrary, "I" remembers Marie as Virgin Mary: "When I remembered Marie from time to time, I now associated her face with the Mexican image of the Virgin Mary she mentioned in her letter" (170); そこで時どき思い出すまり恵さんの姿は、この手紙のメキシコ風なマリア像と結ぶようだ

った (214). We can see here Oe's strategy in naming the heroine of "I"'s narrative Marie with an allusion to Virgin Mary; for "I," Marie is not real, but imaginary or literary.[16] As Gavin sublimates Eula into a literary being in his imagination, "I" imagines Marie as a figure in his religious, or hagiological, narrative.

"I"'s whole narrative seems to be heading toward Marie's conversion. In spite of "I"'s pretense of his sympathy with Marie and Marie's own pretense of sympathy with "I," there is no real sympathy between the two, since the sympathy is always mediated through "I"'s imagination, or his intent to frame Marie's life in his religious narrative. Several years pass after "I" met Marie for the last time, that is, after the night they spent together, and during that period "I" develops his imagination concerning Marie under the disguise of sympathy with her. Although "I"'s wife implicitly criticizes him for his confusing sympathy with imagination, by saying, "You've been letting yourself get too involved with Marie lately, any way. Maybe with her so far away your feelings will settle down a bit" (171), or あなたも、最近はまり恵さんに感情移入をしすぎることがあったから、こうして距離があることで自然な感じに戻れるのじゃない？(215), it is even the more convenient for "I" to keep the distance from Marie, since it is the very source of his imagination. For "I," to imagine Marie as preparing for conversion has become a means to seek his own religious salvation or a healing of his soul. "I"'s religious narrative on Marie has become an expression of his own asceticism. In a sense, Marie's story represents a typical female experience in a predominantly patriarchal society. Marie's life has been manipulated by "I," the male narrator, and turned into a story of conversion. Sarah Gordon says of Flannery O'Connor that "because the patriarchal Church imposes its own set of constraints, many of which have to do with the subordination and denial of flesh, O'Connor would seem not to have found the kind of freedom Virginia Woolf and others advocate for the woman writer" (16). In a similar manner, "I" imposes on Marie a change that is concerned with "denial of flesh," a change from the Marie who used to say, "I want to be free to enjoy my sins,

and that's exactly what I'm doing!" (39) 私は自由に罪を楽しみたい
もの、そして現に楽しんでいるもの！(45) to the Marie who says in her
letter to "I," "*I couldn't think of anything else it would be painful to
give up, so I've decided to swear off sex*" (160) あれこれ思案した末、
今回、もう死ぬまでセックスはしないと、誓うことにしました (201).
Although those remarks are quoted as Marie's own, there is reason to
doubt their authenticity, because they are always/already represented
in "I"'s narrative. In her review of the novel, Tsushima Yuko asserts:
"whereas 'I' makes efforts to record someone's misfortune and its
aftermath as they are, what comes out becomes nothing more than a
'narrative' which is acceptable only to the narrator" (my translation);
ある人物の "突然の不運" と、その後の時間を "僕" という筆者があり
のままを書き記そうとすればするほど、そこに現れるものは、筆者に
納得し得る範囲の "物語" でしかなくなる (288). While Marie refuses
to make the suicide of her two sons "intelligible," "I" keeps trying to
narrate her story as "intelligible" to himself.

Sergio Matsuno visits "I" in Tokyo, and tells him that Marie is
dying from cancer. In one of the photographs sent later from Mexico,
"I" sees Marie sitting up in bed with a V sign made with her fingers,
raised in front of her chest. Because of this V sign, "I" is forced to
feign self-criticism at the end of his narrative. For Matsuno, it would
simply mean Virgin Mary, or the victory over this world. For "I," it is
more likely to represent "vida" in "Parientes de la vida," which,
according to Asao, Marie herself picked up for the title of a film on
Marie's life. Then, in a somewhat roundabout way, "I" also associates
it with the sense of victory—though a humble one—that Marie might
have had when she felt she had been accepted by the Mexican country
women around her as their true friend, that is, "Parientes de la vida."
Yet "I" is not satisfied with his own interpretation. Although "I" has
already written about Marie's life up to the final V sign that Marie has
shown, he is not sure about how Marie views her own life. Then "I"
relies on literature again: "But then recently, one night when I
couldn't sleep, I came across a passage in a paperback edition of
Plutarch where he refers to sadness as an unwelcome 'relative in life'

that nobody ever gets rid of, no matter what situation they're in. I'm now leaning toward this view of it" (189); ところがついこの間、眠りにつけぬまま文庫版で読みつづけていたプルタルコスで、どのような境遇にある者にもつきまとう、あまりありがたくない「人生の親戚」と、悲しみのことを呼びなしている箇所に出あった。いま僕は、こちらの解釈にかたむいている (240). For his second thought, "I" associates Marie's V sign with "Parientes de la vida," and consequently to Plutarch's idea of sadness, or grief. Does "I" mean that Marie should be sorry for the life she has lived? Or does he mean that Marie has already gotten over the grief of her life? Either way, as Gavin reduces Eula's grief to the nights with Flem, "I" misunderstands Marie's grief, if only she feels one, as her final remark on her miserable life.

In "In Lieu of an Epilogue," "I" adds another narrative to the one he has already narrated, and, there, he finally achieves his purpose of turning Marie into a saint who brings to him a religious message. After Marie's death, "I" receives from Asao a video tape which records the scenes concerning the preparation for Marie's burial. "I" also knows that another tape has been confiscated by the customs because it includes Marie's nude body. Based on those fragments, "I" is expected by the crew in Mexico to help edit the film by "arranging a plot / giving words" (my translation) or 物語を作り出し・言葉をあたえる (247). In this added narrative, "I" reveals to readers that, to give the film a plot, he has written a novel in which Marie finally comes to be venerated as saint in the community in Mexico, yet in its final draft he has dropped the details concerning the process in which Marie becomes a saint because he cannot be so sure about "[h]ow a modern saint [is] created" (197); 現代の聖女は、いかに生成して行くものか (250). As he has failed to turn Marie into a saint in the narrative he has narrated before, "I" fails again in the present narrative which he writes as a script for Asao's film, and thinks: "The fact is, though, that because I have no real belief, in any sense of the word, I find it impossible to approach the concept of a saint in my own writing, just as I found it impossible to accept the Counsellor in someone else's work" (198); つまりいかなる意味でも信仰のない僕には、他人の書いたものに新しい教えを説く人を確信できぬと同様、自分の書くものに聖女を容認することもできない(251). After a temporary disappointment, however, "I" thinks of another narrative based on an episode included in Matsuno's diary, a story in which Marie is raped by Macho Mitsuo, who in return is lynched by other men and left out of the community, but, after Marie's death, comes back to dig her grave in cooperation and reconciled with those who lynched him. In this imagined story, "I" finally finds a sign of Marie's sainthood:

死んだ自分の埋葬準備をつうじて、まり恵さんはmacho
ミツオと農場の男たちとの和解を媒介した。それなら
まり恵さんは癌に衰弱しながら最後の生の映像に工夫
をこらして、僕となにものかとの間の媒介をもくろん
だのではないか？誇張と響くかも知れぬのは承知の上
で、僕はむしろmachoミツオを呼び出して痛めつけた
後の、農場の男たちの緊張と恐怖に共振する心の動き
をいだくのである。(258–59)

If, through the preparations for her own burial, the dead Marie could act as a mediator between Mitsuo and the farm, mightn't she also intercede between me and something else, by carefully staging this final image of herself in life? I know how farfetched it may sound, but it makes my heart pound with the same dread those men must have felt after they'd summoned Mitsuo and crippled him. (203–204)

As Gavin, according to Oe, turns Eula/Linda into the female archetype upon which he exerts his imagination, "I" turns Marie into a saint who mediates between him and "something else." What "I" calls "something else" can be some supernatural being, or, more specifically, sympathy with those men who lynched Mitsuo, but, implicitly, it means literature, especially for "I," religious literature.

For "I" as novelist, Marie, the saint, is a Muse who inspires him with
and makes him write religious or hagiological narratives. In this sense,
even if he has failed again and again to draw a religious narrative out
of Marie's life, "I" can still say, "I have already written a novel about
Marie's life, as 'my own story, one acceptable to me'" (204); まり恵
さんの生涯について、僕はすでにひとつの小説を、自分の物語として
了解できるように書いてしまっている (259).

From the perspective of Oe who is critical about his first-person
narrator, however, in "I"'s success is also another failure. Although
"I" thinks that he has turned Marie into a saint, or a mediator, it is Oe
who has turned "I" into a mediator for Marie to present "I" as an
incompetent novelist. In his speech on Faulkner, Oe is purposely
ambiguous concerning whether Gavin is the catalyst or the subject of
his own imagination. Although Gavin believes that he is exerting his
imagination as subject, he can also be nothing but a catalyst which
works for someone else's, say, Eula's or Linda's, imagination. In *An
Echo of Heaven*, Marie speaks, not "I." What the novel presents is not
"I"'s success in assimilating Marie into his religious narrative, but
Marie's success in resisting "I"'s narrative. In this sense, Marie's V
sign represents the victory of a female protagonist over "I," the male
narrator. With her death, Marie leaves everyone, including the narrator, behind. Just as Eula's suicide makes everyone look alike,
Marie's death makes everyone, including Coz, Little Father, Matsuno,
Macho Mitsuo, men who lynched Mitsuo, and "I," look alike. If
Gavin dies in a metaphorical sense when Linda kills her father Flem,
"I" loses his authority as narrator when Marie puts up the V sign in
the video tape. "I" even anticipates that: "For if the customs people
were to return the video of Marie lying there like a Naked Maja
giving the V sign, wouldn't something crucial perhaps happen to me
when I saw it?" (203); 税関から、「裸のマハ」のように素裸でVサイ
ンを示しているまり恵さんのヴィデオが戻って来るとしたら、今度は
それを見るこちらに決定的なことが起るのではないか？(258)

The Subject and the Object

Requiem for a Nun

In *A Quiet Life*, Oe chooses a daughter/sister as the narrator. Although Oe has written novels centered on the father-son relationship modeled on his own relationship with his son Hikari, *A Quiet Life* no longer centers on the father-son relationship, but, instead, foregrounds the daughter-sister figure, enacted by Ma-chan, who is daughter to K, the novelist modeled on Oe, and sister to Eeyore modeled on Hikari.

The novel consists of six short stories. In the first short story, "Shizukana seikatsu" ("A Quiet Life"), which humorously depicts the way the family, especially Ma-chan, copes with Eeyore's being sexually male, we, again, come across a sign of Oe's Faulknerian connection. Instigated, though repelled, by an article in the newspaper reporting an assault on a female student at a camp school by a mentally retarded person, Ma-chan begins to watch her brother, and, one day, finds him standing behind the hedge of a mansion, as if hiding there and aiming at two uniformed school girls coming toward him. Although Ma-chan suffers later from her own suspicion concerning Eeyore's motives in being there, it turns out at the end of the short story that he was listening to Mozart played by the piano in the mansion. Such a figure of mentally retarded person of mature age reminds us of Benjy in *The Sound and the Fury*:

> I could hear them talking. I went out the door and I couldn't hear them, and I went down to the gate, where the girls passed with their booksatchels. They looked at me, walking fast, with their heads turned. I tried to say, but they went on, and I went along the fence, trying to say, and they went faster. Then they were running and I came to the corner of the fence and I couldn't go any further, and I held to the fence, looking after them and trying to say. (Faulkner, *The Sound and the Fury* 51–52)

While the resemblance between Benjy and Eeyore seems obvious, what we are interested in is not concerned with the sexual threats of the mentally retarded, but rather with the subject-object relationship between brother and sister.

We know that the target of Benjy's gaze is not those school girls, but virtually Caddy, who has left home and abandoned him. Although Benjy does not know how to express himself, he is still the subject of speech, one who is "trying to say." On the other hand, Caddy is the object, to be more precise, the absent object, of Benjy's speech; hence the critics' identification of Caddy with the empty signifier. As we have seen in the introduction to the present chapter, however, the recent studies, such as Urgo's and Gwin's, have revealed that Caddy is actually, not symbolically, more eloquent than she appears. What is more, we have rather a curious evidence of Caddy's eloquence; in the "Appendix" written for *The Portable Faulkner*, Faulkner himself spends more words on Caddy than on other characters. Caddy herself does not speak; instead, Melissa Meek, a local librarian, shows Jason and Dilsey Caddy's picture, and speaks for her. Caddy seems to be an absent object again. Moreover, Meek can get nothing in Caddy's favor since Jason has broken with her and Dilsey cannot even see the picture because she is blind. Nevertheless, Caddy's presence over-whelms others, and through them, her life story speaks itself. Susan V. Donaldson argues that, in the "Appendix," Caddy "no longer appears to function as an object under scrutiny situating the gazer and storyteller as male and autonomous," but, on the contrary, "she stands on equal ground, shoulder to shoulder with her fellow Compsons, a figure capable of generating her own narratives" (36). With this, however, Thadious M. Davis disagrees:

> Ultimately, Caddy remains icon, a visual symbol of masculine desire and longing, of male need and loss. In part, the iconography resonates with the author's sense of his own perceived, diminished ability to participate in con-temporary history. In standing beside a machine, "an

open powerful expensive chromium-trimmed sports car,"
and a German officer, Caddy is appended to both the
mechanistic world of power and to the militaristic world of
power seeking race and class dominance. Her stance is a
reiteration of the disruptiveness marking her presence in
and absence from the novel proper. In the Appendix,
however, she is no longer the disruptive feminine voice that
Gwin identifies in the novel proper. (246)

Then, is Caddy a subject or an object? This is the very question that
Oe asks in *A Quiet Life*. If we can say that Caddy's voice resonates in
Oe's novel, it is in terms of her being ambiguously positioned be-
tween subjectivity and objectivity.

In the wake of structuralist way of thinking, many of us share
the knowledge that the subject, or consequently the subject-object
relationship, is the effect of structure, especially of language. The
structuralist reduction of Caddy to either subject or object—be it
called an empty signifier, the object of male gazes, or the subject of
her own narratives on equal terms with other male narrators—works
as long as it assumes the precedence of structure, or language, that
precedes its effort. Luce Irigaray, however, teaches us to think otherwise:

To be sure language stays in us as we dwell in it. We can
believe that it is our source, and that we cannot go out of its
horizon. But this is not exactly the case. We live before
speaking and our own origin is on this side of an already
existing language. Saying ourselves cannot happen without
transgressing the already learned forms. Our existence, our
hyle—body and soul—are irreducible to the making of a
technique whatever it may be, including a technique of
language and, even more, irreducible to the effects that this
techné has already produced starting from another life, from
another *hyle*, than our own. (*The Way of Love* 84–85)

Simply to expect Caddy to speak, we have to paradoxically deny her
subjectivity, because that means simply to expect Caddy to learn the
techné of language, or, in other words, to play the role of a subject
that is cast by structure. Irigaray does not necessarily discourage our
being subjects; rather, being a subject means more than just to be
a transmitter of what pretends to be neutral and universal—say
language—in a culture, or, in particular, to be an "exchanger of words,
as he is an exchanger of goods or . . . of women" (62) in a patriarchal
culture. In order not to reduce Caddy to either subject or object in the
structure which the subject is potentially always male and the object
is female, we should expect her to speak another language in which
the subject-object relationship no longer rules. Against monologue,
that is, the language based on the subject-object relationship, Irigaray
advocates dialogue, which even demands a reformation of grammar:

> Privileging the use of verbs which take a direct object
> encouraging the subject-object relation to the detriment of
> the subject-subject relation, which needs a little more
> indirection in order to avoid the reduction of the other to an
> object of one's own. In dialogue, proximity, as well as the
> proper, are irreducible to a certain form of appropriation—
> not making one's own is imperative for remaining two. That
> sometimes demands certain transformation of discourse. "I
> love to you" is more unusual than "I love you," but respects
> the two more: I love to who you are, to what you do,
> without reducing you to an object of my love. (60)

Throughout both *The Sound and the Fury* and the "Appendix,"
Caddy's voice is never heard directly; it is always filtered through the
other consciousness. This is not, however, the sign of her being
always treated as object; rather, it should be taken as a sign of
indirection which accompanies the language in which two remains
two, and which sustains the subject-subject relationship; hence
the recent attempts to listen to Caddy's voice in those seemingly

monologic texts.

Requiem for a Nun treats, rather directly, the question of such a new language as Irigaray advocates. In the play, Temple says that she takes Nancy, whom she calls "ex-dope-nigger whore," out of the gutter to nurse her children, because Nancy "was the only animal in Jefferson that spoke Temple Drake's language" (136). She also says that what she needed was "[s]omebody to talk to, as we all seem to need, want, have to have, not to converse with you nor even agree with you, but just to keep quiet and listen" (137). Here Temple seems to be near Irigaray, who says that "[t]he silence of a between-two, the listening to the other, which to be sure cuts into a plenitude founded on the same but does not signify for all that an alienation, are ways which contribute toward a dialectical process of which the movement is assured by the difference between the subjects" (99). Although Irigaray's idea of dialogue is basically conceived to be built between two subjects of different sexes—that is, beyond sexual difference—, we can assume that what Temple expected between herself and Nancy is the same kind of ideal dialogue as Irigaray conceives, a dialogue which Temple should have had with her husband Gowan Stevens. To build a dialogue between herself and Nancy, Temple has to overcome the racial difference, as well as the difference in social rank. However, Temple herself betrays such an ideal. At the end of the play, we hear from Temple that Nancy has lost her own baby, while it was still in her belly because "the man kicked you in the stomach" (240). Just as Temple has expected something in Nancy her confidante, Nancy also has expected the same in Temple and so she has confided to her her most painful memory. Yet Temple betrays Nancy's confidence by not understanding her pain. By deciding to elope with Pete, Temple discloses her inattentiveness to the connection between Nancy's loss of her unborn baby and her abandoning her own two children, especially the six-month-old baby. In the flashback enacted in Act Two, Scene ii, Nancy asks Temple, rather directly, if she will really abandon the children:

Nancy

—I'm talking about two little children—

Temple

I said, hush.

Nancy

I cant hush. I'm going to ask you one more time. Are
you going to do it?

Temple

Yes!

Nancy

Maybe I am ignorant. You got to say it out in words yourself,
so I can hear them. Say, I'm going to do it.

Temple

You heard me. I'm going to do it.

Nancy

Money or no money.

Temple

Money or no money.

Nancy

Children or no children.

(Temple doesn't answer)

To leave one with a man that's willing to believe the child
aint got no father, willing to take the other one to a man that
dont even want no children—

(They stare at one another)

If you can do it, you can say it.

Temple

Yes! Children or no children! Now get out of here. Take
your part of that money, and get out. Here— (163–64)

Nancy urges Temple to say it, whereas Temple hesitates to.
Apparently, there is a silence here. However, the silence to which
Temple sticks is not Irigaray's silence, a silence which creates a
dialogue. There is an irony here. Indeed, Nancy urges Temple to say

it. But once Temple says it, that is, says yes, that ends the dialogue that should be created, because what Nancy really wants Temple to do is to say no, or to remain silent. In fact, Temple says yes, and that ends the dialogue; Nancy goes out of the room and kills the six-month-old baby, whom Temple has abandoned *de facto*.[17]

Having failed to build a dialogue with Nancy, that is, having lost a chance to be in a subject-subject relationship with the other, Temple remains to be an object in the subject-object relationship with Nancy, her husband Gowan, and Gavin Stevens. After the sentence of death on Nancy is passed, Temple leaves for California, and stays there for four months until she receives a telegraph from Gavin, which reminds her that Nancy's execution is a week away. Back home, a day before Nancy's execution, Temple visits the Governor's office with Gavin at two o'clock in the morning not to save Nancy, because it is too late, but, in Gavin's words, "for [Temple's] right to sleep at night" (77), and, in Temple's paraphrase, "for the good of my soul—if I have one?" (78) Here, we see the same Gavin as we have seen in *The Town* and *The Mansion*. Before they come to the Governor's office, Gavin has told Temple that "[t]he past is never dead. It's not even past" (80). In the Governor's office, Gavin urges Temple to narrate, yet later Gavin himself narrates Temple's past, which begins with the night described in *Sanctuary*, the night eight years before when she and her future husband Gowan wrecked a car and stopped by the moon-shiner's house where Popeye lived. While they are speaking with the Governor, Gowan is hiding behind the door (or somewhere off stage) and eavesdropping on their conversation. Gowan appears on the stage from the beginning of Scene iii of Act Two and sits in the Governor's chair instead of the Governor, though Temple does not recognize him until later in the scene. It is Gavin who set up the situation. Gavin's purpose is to let Temple confess her sin in front of her husband, who, as invisible, is implicitly equated by Gavin with God, or at least God's agent on earth. For Gavin, Temple's sin lies in her being the same Temple Drake as she was eight years before, that is, the Temple Drake who once betrayed her boy friend Gowan and loved Red and now has betrayed her husband Gowan again and tried to elope with Red's brother Pete. Gavin calls such a Temple Drake the "truth":

Temple

What do you want then? What more do you want?

Stevens

Temple Drake.

Temple

(quick, harsh, immediate)

No. Mrs Gowan Stevens.

Stevens

(implacable and calm)

Temple Drake. The truth. (76)

Just as he tries to fix Eula in the image of "*was*" and form Linda's mind in *The Town* and *The Mansion*, Gavin tries to fix Temple in her past and form her mind through repentance before her husband/God. When Gavin refers to God, therefore, he is talking to Gowan behind the door: "And since God—if there was one—must be aware of that, then she too would bear her side of the bargain by not demanding on Him a second time since He—if there was one—would at least play fair, would be at least a gentleman" (142). The phrase "if there was one" sounds like "Are you listening, Gowan?"

This is far from what Irigaray calls dialogue that is based on the subject-subject relationship. It is true that Temple partially narrates her past, and, in this sense, she is the subject of her narrative; but, from the beginning, it is planned by Gavin that she should confess her sin and be the object of, as she calls it, Gavin's "plants" (173). Temple speaks, while she is heard by someone to whom she does not intend to be speaking. She appears to be the subject, but in fact she is the object. In Gavin's understanding, Temple's life, or her marriage with Gowan, is reduced to forgiveness and gratitude:

> The first thing was the gratitude. . . . Because it was not
> long before she discovered, realized, that she was going to
> spend a good part of the rest of her days (nights too) being
> forgiven for it; in being not only constantly reminded—well,
> maybe not specifically reminded, but say made—kept—
> aware of it in order to be forgiven for it so that she might be
> grateful to the forgiver, but in having to employ more and
> more of what tact she had . . . to make the gratitude—in
> which she had probably had as little experience as she had
> had with patience—acceptable to meet with, match, the high
> standards of the forgiver. (139)

Temple is the subject of gratitude to Gowan, but, at the same time, she is the object of his forgiveness. In this subject-object relationship, there is no true reciprocity, or what Irigaray calls "proximity," which exists in the subject-subject relationship. As Gavin tactfully describes it, Temple's gratitude, or even her subjectivity, depends on Gowan's forgiveness. In order to gain her subjectivity, Temple has to beg Gowan for his forgiveness. This is exactly the life from which Temple tried to escape by eloping with Pete, and to which Gavin now tries to send her back. What Temple sees in her future is the repetition of the days of gratitude and forgiveness: "it can go on, tomorrow and tomorrow and tomorrow, forever and forever and forever" (180). After Gavin's sermon, however, what Temple really means here is "yesterday and yesterday and yesterday, the past and the past and the past." At the end of her confession in front of three male listeners or priests, that is, Gavin, Gowan, and the Governor, Temple feels quite at a loss: "To save my soul—if I have a soul. If there is a God to save it—a God who wants it—" (182).

In Act Three, Temple meets Nancy in jail. This is the last chance for Temple to build the subject-subject relationship, a dialogue, with Nancy. But she fails. Nancy tells Temple to "believe" (234, 241, 243), but Temple does not know what Nancy means by "believe." Temple once asked Nancy to stay with her and nurse her children, because she "was the only animal in Jefferson that spoke Temple Drake's language," but it turns out here that Nancy's language is different from Temple's. Temple tells Nancy to hush, so Nancy hushes: "All right. I've hushed. Because it's all right. I can get low for Jesus too. I can get low for Him too" (234–35). Nancy hushes because Temple, her white mistress, tells her to. Then, sarcastically, Nancy tells Temple that she can "get low" for Temple because she can also "get low" for Jesus. As a black woman and an ex-whore picked up out of the gutter, Nancy knows how to "get low" in several ways: she can "get low" for the white in general; she can "get low" for men in a sexual sense; she can "get low" for men in general, that is, for patriarchy. Although Temple criticizes Nancy's sexual allusion to Jesus for blasphemy, she understands, or at least she thinks she understands, Nancy's sarcasm, because, after Gavin's sermon, she is also enclosed in the cage of patriarchal language. However, Nancy tells Temple something different: "Jesus is a man too. He's got to be. Menfolks listens to somebody because of what he says. Women dont. They dont care what he said. They listens because of what he is" (235). By "women" here, Nancy means women like herself, not Temple. By "menfolks" and "women," then, Nancy means more than the sexual difference; she means the difference of race, and of class as well. Nancy believes in Jesus in spite of her sarcastic view of him as a man, not because of what he says but of what he is, that is, because of his being there to accept her belief, or to provide her with an object for her belief. To Nancy, what Jesus says, or in what language he speaks, has only a secondary importance; what is most important is that an object of her belief, which makes her the subject of belief, is given to her in whatever language she happens to speak, even if it is the language of patriarchy, especially of white patriarchy. Of course, Nancy's belief is ideologically determined, and in that sense, Nancy is a subject only in a subject-object relationship given by a culture. But as Temple asks in the quote above, who can challenge it? This seems to be the very question asked by Faulkner throughout the prose parts of the play.

What is depicted through the prose parts of the play that precede the dramatic parts is the process in which a male-centered culture—the center of which is the jail, which is likened to the "old mirror" or the "patriarch" (191)—is formed. In a way that reminds us of Foucault's study of power or of Althusser's study of institutions (Ideological State Apparatus), those prose parts reveal how a culture comes to enclose the land, limit the freedom of the people, and, more importantly, repress the feminine, which begins with and is represented by Mohataha the native American matriarch. The process culminates in the prologue to Act Three, which is entitled "The Jail," with the figure of Cecilia Farmer, a turnkey's daughter, who until taken away by a husband from Alabama after the Civil War sits beside the window of her father's house (jail) and keeps watching the outside. Both Temple and Nancy are the descendants and the embodiments of those repressed female figures in the past; especially, Nancy is so, because she is actually confined in jail. When Nancy says, "I can get low for Him," therefore, she is reverberating Cecilia's words from the jail, *"Listen, stranger; this was myself: this was I"* (225), which echo in the mind of a stranger—the reader—who happens to pass through Jefferson and remembers her name inscribed on the windowpane of the jail.

Temple's case is a little different from Nancy's. Although Temple tries to take Nancy's side, she cannot become one of those women who "listens because of what he is." Jesus, who speaks to Nancy, does not speak to Temple: "Then let Him talk to me. I can get low for Him too, if that's all He wants, demands, asks. I'll do anything He wants if He'll just tell me what to do. No: how to do it. I know what to do, what I must do, what I've got to do. But how?" (235) Again and again, Nancy tells Temple to "believe," but Temple does not know how. Temple does not understand what Nancy means, not only because she is skeptical, but also because Nancy's language is not hers. In Act Two, Scene iii, there is a long line of Temple, which looks almost like a monologue. In the line, Temple speaks of black prisoners, especially of their hands, not eyes, seen between the bars, which

> can see the shape of the plow or hoe or axe before daylight
> comes; and even in the dark, without even having to turn on
> the light, can not only find the child, the baby—not her
> child but yours, the white one—but the trouble and
> discomfort too—the hunger, the wet didy, the unfastened
> safety-pin—and see to remedy it. (170)

Then, Temple speaks of Rider, who appears in "Pantaloon in Black"
included in *Go Down, Moses*. Temple quotes what Rider says at the
end of the short story almost word for word: "Look like I just cant
quit thinking. Look like I just cant quit" (171). Here Temple comes
close to speaking Nancy's language. Moreover, in Act Three, when
she recalls and mentions Nancy's child who was killed while she is
pregnant, Temple comes closer to Nancy's language. Yet this is the
closest Temple can come; even if she can understand the tenderness or
loyalty of black nurses who take care of white babies or the sorrow of
Rider who has lost his wife after six months of marriage, Temple
cannot understand why Nancy killed her baby.

Temple leaves the baby because she can believe that Nancy, a
black woman who should be able to find a white baby even in the
dark, will take care of it. But Nancy won't. Instead, she kills the baby,
and by doing so, she turns it into a sufferer, like her own unborn baby
which was conceived by somebody unspecified and kicked to death
by somebody whom she could not tell whether he was its father or not.
Here is the crucial difference between Temple and Nancy: Temple can
count on her black nurse to take care of her baby, while Nancy knows
no one except Jesus to entrust her dead, though unborn, baby.[18] In
her unborn baby's death lies the basis of Nancy's belief. Because it
suffered, she can also suffer.

Nancy is a sufferer herself. Nancy is going to die for Temple. As
we have seen, Temple has committed a sin toward Gowan/God.
Although it is a sin in the eyes of Gowan/God, or Gavin, it is also a
sin toward her children, and it is Temple's sin toward her children that
Nancy is going to atone for. By killing the baby which Temple

deserted, Nancy has taken Temple's sin upon herself. While stressing the sincerity of Nancy's will to sacrifice herself, Noel Polk argues that her means to do so is unjustifiable: "Even granting Nancy the right to sacrifice herself if she chooses, we still must hold that she has absolutely no right to take the life of that little baby" (*Faulkner's Requiem for a Nun* 141). Overall, referring to the conflict between Alyosha and Ivan Karamazov in *The Brothers Karamazov*, Polk reduces the relationship between Temple and Nancy to the conflict between Temple's skepticism and Nancy's faith: "as I've tried to argue, the meaning of *Requiem for a Nun* lies much closer to Temple's anguished questioning in Act III than to Nancy's serene untroubled faith" (218). We should not forget, however, that Nancy's faith originates in the same anguish as Temple has—that is, the anguish caused by the death of a baby—and, what is more, Nancy is still in the same anguish. Nancy believes in Jesus because she is in anguish. She has acquired the faith because she has lost her unborn baby. It seems as if Nancy's belief is in itself an anguish and she needs the belief in order to keep the anguish alive. We see here a mechanism in which a painful memory, or a painful experience itself, is willingly repeated: by getting her unborn baby killed, Nancy passively and uncannily experiences Jesus' passion; then, by killing Temple's baby, Nancy actively repeats Jesus' passion with Temple's baby; moreover, herself becoming a sacrifice for Temple, Nancy repeats Jesus' passion herself. Nancy is like the child described by Freud in *Beyond the Pleasure Principle*, who reenacts his mother's disappearance and return by throwing the wooden reel.

If we still want to ask why Nancy killed the baby, we should say that she wanted to die. The experience of Rider is parallel to Nancy's. Rider is lynched after being arrested for killing a white. As Temple quotes it, Rider says in jail, "Look like I just cant quit thinking. Look like I just cant quit." It seems as if Rider killed the white person so that he would get lynched, and by getting killed, he could forget the traumatic experience of his wife's death. It seems also, however, that he killed the white person so that he would get lynched, and by getting lynched, he could actively repeat what had passively happened to him. If so, he is not trying to "quit thinking," but, on the contrary, trying to keep recalling the pain of losing his wife. Similarly, Nancy is not trying to erase the memory of losing her unborn baby, but, on the contrary, trying to remember it. By remembering it, Nancy is trying to live and die peacefully, because for her, though paradoxically, peace of mind lies in her suffering and the meaning of her life in her sacrificial death.

In the play, Nancy does not mention her lost baby; Nancy seems rather hesitant to talk about it. It is Temple who mentions it. In Nancy's psyche, it is repressed because it is painful, though it comes back again and again. To talk about it, Nancy has to find another expression, hence her belief. Uncannily asked by Gavin if "you have got to sin," Nancy answers as if talking about not her, but someone else: "You aint *got* to. You cant help it. And He knows that too" (238). "He" means at once Jesus and Nancy's lost baby. Nancy cannot help sinning or suffering, and her ultimate goal for the sinning and suffering is to be saved, that is, to die. Nancy does not say so, because her desire to die is suppressed in her unconscious. Instead of talking about her unborn baby and her own death wish, she keeps saying that she believes.

On behalf of Nancy, however, Temple mentions Rider, and later, in front of Nancy, her unborn baby. Curiously enough, we see here the closest tie, or the like of dialogue, between Temple and Nancy. Here is the point where Temple comes closest to Nancy, but, at the same time, this is the point which crucially separates Temple from Nancy. By mentioning Nancy's lost baby on behalf of Nancy herself, Temple speaks Nancy's language. However, this does not lead her to understanding both Nancy and herself in the same language. Temple indeed comes close to understanding the connection between them. But she fails. What Temple misses most is that Nancy's destiny is her own. Nancy is at once the subject and the object of suffering, in the sense that she passively suffers a traumatic experience at the outset and actively repeats it later. Now, getting her baby killed, Temple suffers the same initiating trauma as Nancy suffered. But, for now, Temple does not see her future. Whereas Gavin confines her to her past, Nancy foretells in Temple's future a repetition of such an initial trauma, a repetition which resembles what Freud called "compulsion to repeat" in *Beyond the Pleasure Principle*.

At the end of their meeting, Temple expresses her fear and suspicion to Nancy: "Even if there is one and somebody waiting in it to forgive me, there's still tomorrow and tomorrow. And suppose tomorrow and tomorrow, and then nobody there, nobody waiting to forgive me—" (242-43). Nancy simply tells Temple to believe. Then, Temple asks, "Believe what, Nancy?" (243) and Nancy tells her to believe again. Temple seems quite at a loss; her skepticism makes her so. Temple has already been suffering and, in this sense, she is the subject of her suffering; but, at the same time, she is the object of her suffering, because, like Nancy, she passively suffered the suffering in the beginning. Suffering, or "compulsion to repeat," makes one at the same time a subject and an object. However, if we follow Althusser's Marxist interpretation of Freud and Lacan, such a "compulsion to repeat," in which one becomes a subject and/or an object, is in itself an effect of a structure that is ideologically determined by the dominant bourgeois patriarchal culture.[19] In this sense, Temple shares an experience with Nancy; only she is too skeptical about what she is or where she is. Nancy's language is centered on Jesus' passion; for Nancy, suffering means belief in "Him," whether or not He is a man. In Temple's language, suffering means, as Gavin has led her to think, a belief in him, a man, that is, her husband; it signifies simply the days of forgiveness and gratitude in the male-centered culture or the Gowan/God-centered life.[20] Confined to a structure, Temple fails to build an Irigarayian dialogue. Only her skepticism is left to her.

A Quiet Life

It is hard to believe that Oe did not refer to such a figure of Temple when he created Ma-chan in *Shizukana seikatsu*, or *A Quiet Life*. In Oe's novel, Ma-chan suffers from the idea that either she herself or his brother Eeyore has been made a sacrifice for their father K. This resembles the situation in which Temple suffers from the idea that both her own baby, which was killed by Nancy, and Nancy, who killed the baby, have sacrificed their lives for her. Moreover, Ma-chan resembles Temple in the sense that she is under the influence of her father's religious language. In Faulkner's play, Temple feels at a loss, bound at the same time by Gavin's patriarchal religion, in which she is led to confess her sin before her husband/God, and by Nancy's religion of suffering, in which she is involved in the repetition of Jesus' passion. In both cases, Temple is prevented from having a dialogue, or a language based on the subject-subject relationship. Similarly, for Ma-chan, to think herself or Eeyore as sacrifice means to be captivated by the strong influence of the language of K, a novelist, and to be forced to remain in the position of an object in the father-daughter, author-reader, teacher-pupil relationship.

As a whole, *A Quiet Life* is concerned with the motif of sacrifice. Invited by the University of California to be a writer-in-residence, K leaves Tokyo for California, and his wife accompanies him. In Tokyo, Eeyore, Ma-chan, and their brother O-chan are left. For K, the reason for going to California is not only professional, but also spiritual or even religious. K is in what he calls a "pinch." According to Mr. Shigeto, K's friend and Eeyore's music teacher, K's present pinch is triggered by a lecture called "The Prayers of a Faithless Man," which he has given at a woman's university. After the lecture was televised, K receives a letter from a Catholic priest whom he respects, and is told that he is "already on the church's side" もう教会の側の人 (69).[21] This letter shocks K, who believes to have always been a person on "this side" こちら側 (69). Mr. Shigeto suggests to Ma-chan that K decided to go to California to think over the question of his faith-like, yet faithless, prayers; to do so, he had to separate himself from Eeyore, the life with whom, or whose difficulty, had given others the impression that he had been devoting himself to "matters of the soul" 魂のこと (65, 66). Mr. Shigeto even assumes that there is a possibility that, to acquire a true faith, K might be thinking of abandoning everything, especially Eeyore, according to his childhood experience of reading an article about St Francis of Assisi, through which he came to believe that "in order to do the matters of the soul, he needed to abandon everything and have a religious awakening"; 魂のことをするためにはすべてを棄てて発心しなければならない (65). Mr. Shigeto's assumption is based on the fact that Eeyore has titled his piano piece "Sutego," or an abandoned child. It turns out later, however, at the end of the second short story titled "Kono wakusei no sutego" ("Abandoned Children of This Planet"), that the full title of Eeyore's piece is "Sutego o tasukeru," or rescuing an abandoned child. Eeyore has probably in mind the abandoned baby that was found in the park which he and his co-workers at the welfare workshop clean every Tuesday; but there still remains a doubt for Ma-chan that her father has abandoned Eeyore, and her and O-chan as well, and sacrificed them for his own peace of mind.

As a novelist, K is obsessed with the literary images of sacrifice, and through his literary influence, Ma-chan is also obsessed with the idea. Although she has never read her father's writings, she has been under her father's literary influence for quite a long time. In "Shosetsu no kanashimi" ("Sadness of the Novel"), Ma-chan recalls an episode about reading *Momo* by Ende, whom she calls a "writer who mediates between Father and me" 私と父を媒介してくれる作家 (176):

> 父との関係で、私に良い感情があるひとつは、エンデ
> の『モモ』を読んだ時の思い出だ。中学のクラスで課
> 題図書として読み、誰もが昂奮しているのを見て、国
> 語の先生が私たちの幼稚な過熱に水をかける必要を感
> じられたのか、──しかし、ひとりの少女が全世界を
> 救うというようなことは、実際には起りえないんだね、
> といわれた。(175)

> I remember when I read Ende's *Momo*; a memory that makes me feel good about my relationship with Father.

I read it as a required reading at my middle school. Every one got excited, but probably feeling the need to calm us—our childish enthusiasm—down, our teacher said, "But one little girl saving the whole world . . . in reality, it just can't happen."

If we recall Mr. Compson in *The Sound and the Fury* here, this teacher's cynicism should be K's. On the contrary, however, K is more like Gavin and Nancy who together try to teach Temple the importance of sacrifice: Gavin says, "The salvation of the world is man's suffering. Is that it?" and Nancy answers, "Yes, sir" (Faulkner, *Requiem for a Nun* 237). K says to Ma-chan:

> マーちゃんよ、ひとりの少女が全世界を救うということは、むしろたびたびあったと思うよ。・・・マーちゃんな、きみが全世界を救うことになってしまったらさ、覚えておいて話してくれよ。僕に話すのがおっくうだったら、イーヨーにね。かれはモモ以上に良い聞き手だからね。(175–76)

> Ma-chan, I'd rather think that one little girl has often saved the world, though we haven't had the chance to hear about her. Ma-chan, if you end up saving the world someday, remember what you did and tell us about it. If you feel embarrassed to tell me, tell Eeyore. He's a better listener than Momo.

Momo does not necessarily sacrifice herself, yet, for Ma-chan, who since her childhood has seen her father "to much preoccupied with Eeyore to be really interested in either me or O-chan" イーヨーに夢中で、私にもオーちゃんにも本当には関心を持っていない (42–43), K's words sound as if she should suffer and sacrifice herself for the sake of her brother, and ultimately her father. In this sense, K's praise of Momo includes an irony. K hardly sounds different from Gavin, who encourages Temple to sacrifice herself and save her soul, that is, her life with Gowan. Just as Gavin urges Temple to confess in front of the Governor and Gowan, K urges Ma-chan to tell her story of saving the world either to himself or Eeyore. In our context, "sav[ing] the world by retrieving time" in K's words implicitly means Ma-chan's possible spiritual regeneration, like the one expected from Temple or even Caddy, which is supposed to bring a peace in a patriarchal household.

Furthermore, this is the very question that Ma-chan asks K after reading Ende's *The Neverending Story*, that is, the question of death and rebirth:

> 父と話すことの正直いって苦手な私が、手に持った『はてしない物語』に励まされる気がして、尋ねるだけのことは尋ねようとしていた。死んでしまえばなにも無くなってしまうのが恐い。お友達は、生まれる前、ずっと幾億年も、なにも無かったのが恐いといってるよ。――・・・そうかい？困ったねえ。僕自身いまはもうそのことをあまり考えないけれど、年をとるにつれて、ゼロになることの恐さに鈍感になっているだけで、マーちゃんを勇気づけられる知恵があるわけじゃないんだよ。人類の歴史、というような規模でいえば、死んだ人間の再生ということはいつでも考えられて来たわけだけれど・・・ (182)

To tell the truth, I am not good at communicating with Father. But encouraged by *The Neverending Story* in my hands, I dared try to tell him: "I'm afraid of becoming nothing after death. I also have a friend who says she is afraid of the idea that she had been nothing for billions of years before she was born." "Well," he said, "it's too bad. I don't think about it anymore. Not that I have any wisdom to encourage you with, but that as I grew older I have become more insensitive to the fear of becoming zero. If you look at

> human history, though, the idea of reincarnation has always
> been with us."

The question for Ma-chan is who is the sacrifice for whom, or whose
death is for whose rebirth. To this, K tries to answer by suggesting
that individual death is for the sake of the whole human being. What
is implied in K's answer is, again, that Ma-chan should sacrifice
herself, because as an individual she is nothing. Against this, Ma-chan
resists: "Even if you reincarnated, . . . if you remember nothing of
your previous life, it's the same as your having become nothing, isn't
it?; 再生しても、以前のことはすっかり忘れてしまっているのなら、
いまの自分は無くなってしまうのと同じでしょう？ (182)

Although Ma-chan acknowledges that her "fear of death is
connected with Father's crying over Dr. W's death" (148), her fear of
death is different from K's: for K, death is a death in history, but, for
Ma-chan, death is a death in nothing. K also used to be afraid of
dying, or turning into nothing, especially after Dr. W's death, but now,
he says that he has become "insensitive to the fear of becoming zero."
As a patriarch and a successful author, that is, as the subject of history,
K can believe in the history which lasts even after his personal death.
On the other hand, Ma-chan cannot believe in such an idea of history,
because she is merely an object, or a sacrifice which is expected to act
only within a particular patriarchal household. For Ma-chan, therefore,
to save the world, or to sacrifice herself, does not mean to become a
savior of the world. It rather means to dedicate her life to the
household to which she belongs; hence her identification with Albion,
not Jesus, in the passage from Blake's "Jerusalem" translated and
quoted in K's short story. After reading the passage in which Jesus
sacrifices himself for Albion, Ma-chan has a dream in which she "is
standing in front of the 'Tree of Life' in Albion's stead. Even in a
dream, [she] can't see Christ himself because He is too awesome for
her eyes to see"; アルビオンのかわりに自分が「生命の木」の前に立
っている夢を見た・・・。夢のなかでもイエス自体は私たちの眼に畏
れおおいからかよく見えないで (185). Although she has identi-

fied herself with Momo, who saves the world, Ma-chan never dreams
of standing in Jesus' position, because Momo is a girl and, as Nancy
in *Requiem for a Nun* says, Jesus is a man. In her compulsion to
repeat, in spite of her awareness of Jesus' gender, Nancy can believe
in Jesus and wish to repeat his suffering; Temple cannot. Ma-chan is
another Temple, who feels at a loss how to believe, or even what to
believe. In her dream, standing at the foot of Christ, and herself being
an Albion, Ma-chan also sees a cherub, which is Eeyore, floating in
the sky. Under K's literary influence, Ma-chan dreams of Christ,
Albion, and the cherub, but the dream is nothing but a projection of
her family.

Between the reflections on Ende and Blake, however, Ma-chan
inserts in her narrative a passage which makes the reader suspect that
what is narrated here, including the overall humorous tone that hints a
later reconciliation with her father, is, after all, a life which she has
already left behind, or even denied. Rather abruptly, Ma-chan expresses her present, somewhat nihilistic, view of death and rebirth,
which has nothing to do with human history, sacrifice, or saving the
world:

> ところが現在の私は再生ということを考える時、いま
> の自分のことはすっかり忘れた新しい人間に——また
> は新しい動物か植物、ともかくも生命のあるものに
> ——なってしまうことが好ましいと感じている。この
> 自分を忘れてしまうのなら、なにも無くなることと同
> じだ、とは感じていない。むしろ、再生した後は前の
> 生のことを覚えていないし、この生のうちにあるかぎ
> りは、次にどのようなものとして再生するのか思いつ
> かないというのが気持が良い、と感じている。(182–83)

> However, when I think of rebirth now, I feel it's better to
> become a new person—even an animal, a plant, or anything
> with life—who has completely forgotten who I am now. I
> don't feel that if I forget who I am now, I become nothing.

Rather, I feel that I will be comfortable if, after being born
again, I won't remember anything of my previous life, and
even during this lifetime, I never know what I will be in my
next life.

Because of this aimlessness, this-worldliness, or the nihilism which
says yes to the eternal recurrence of the same, Ma-chan looks all the
more like Temple, who willy-nilly, yet only temporarily, belongs to
her husband's house. What is more, here we can even hear an echo of
Eula's "You just are," and also of Faulkner, who said in the Jean Stein
interview that "time is a fluid condition which has no existence
except in the momentary avatars of individual people."

Basically, Ma-chan fails to narrate her narrative on her own.
Although she is the narrator, her narrative is permeated by her father's
language. Whether she calls Eeyore an "antichrist" rather than Christ
in "Annai-nin" ("The Guide [*Stalker*]") or a "nobody" なんでもない
人 (169) rather than "somebody special" 特別な人 or a "mysterious
and interesting person" 不思議な面白い人 (170) in "Jido-ningyo no
akumu" ("A Robot's Nightmare"), Ma-chan is simply reversing her
father's view of Eeyore, and, by so doing, repeating the way in which
her father describes Eeyore. However, Ma-chan sometimes slips out
of her father's influence and inserts a space like the one seen above.
In those rare occasions, Ma-chan is narrating in the present of
narration, not in the present of the events narrated. If we call such a
space as inserted by a female character/narrator into Father's
patriarchal language the feminine, what we see here resembles what
Derrida, in *Spurs: Nietzsche's Styles/Éperons: Les Styles de Nietzsche*,
calls woman, that is, *écriture* (writing), or the work of *différance*
(difference + deferment):

Nietzsche's writing is compelled to suspend truth between
the tenter-hooks of quotation marks—and suspended there
with truth is—all the rest. Nietzsche's writing is an inscription of the truth. And such an inscription, even if we

do not venture so far as to call it the feminine itself, is indeed the feminine "operation." Because woman is (her own) writing, style must return to her. In other words, it could be said that if style were a man (much as the penis, according to Freud is the "normal prototype of fetishes"), then writing would be a woman. (57)

In *A Quiet Life*, style is K's language, and writing is Ma-chan's narration, or her attempts to paraphrase or even divert K's words. Whereas K's style claims authority, Ma-chan's writing reveals that the authority depends on the effect of her paraphrasing or diversion, that is, her *différance*. Whereas K's style pretends to represent the world, Ma-chan's writing reveals that his world is the effect of her representation, that is, her narration. Although Ma-chan is the narrator, she narrates under the influence of her father's language. However, whereas K's style pretends to show itself, Ma-chan's writing lurks in it and reveals itself as an "operation" which allows K's style to show itself.

We can recall here that Temple has also failed to narrate her past with her own language. Temple's language is revised and reformed by Gavin's language, which is even different from Nancy's. In a sense, they all share an identical language, because they share the same bourgeois patriarchal white ideology. However, Temple's dissatisfaction with Gavin's or Nancy's language marks a default in the structure. It is true that because of her dissatisfaction, Temple is lost at the end of the play. However, because of dissatisfaction, Temple keeps asking, and because of her dissatisfaction, Gavin and Nancy have to speak up and pretend to agree on the ideas of belief, suffering, and salvation. Gavin and Nancy are styles, while Temple is what Derrida calls writing. Temple's dissatisfaction lurks in the language of Gavin and Nancy. Temple is lost, but she is always there. Although, as we have seen, Temple has failed to have what Irigaray calls dialogue, or the subject-subject relationship, because she has always been in the ideologically determined subject-object relationship, she at least suggests a disruption in such a monologic language of the subject-object relationship.

Temple, however, ends up being caught in the subject-object relationship. On the other hand, pretending to stay in the subject-object relationship, Ma-chan asks a weird question: who is actually speaking? While caught in the subject-object relationship of the father-daughter, author-reader, teacher-pupil relationship, Ma-chan nevertheless inserts her space in her father's language by paraphrasing and diverting his words. In somewhat a similar manner that Derrida calls writing a woman, Irigaray calls such an "operation" within Father's language "femininity":

> Femininity is part and parcel of the patriarchal order. Woman is hidden in the thought of the father. When she gives birth to herself fully equipped—even with weapons. She is veiled, her beauty hidden. Only the shape appears anymore. Therefore, not the woman. She would no longer touch herself. Only the face sees/is seen. And the voice clearly expresses the father's wishes, which she translates into words all men—all citizens—can hear. (*Marine Lover of Friedrich Nietzsche* 96)

What Ma-chan is doing throughout her narrative is exactly this: to express her "father's wishes and translate them into words" so that others "can hear" them.

In the last short story, "Ie to shite no nikki" ("Diary as Home"), Ma-chan narrates an episode concerning Mr. Arai, who volunteers as Eeyore's swimming coach. Answering her letter to her mother in California, in which Ma-chan has written about Mr. Arai, K immediately writes a letter and tells her not to see him with no one else around. Ma-chan hears from Mr. and Mrs. Shigeto about a murder case in which Mr. Arai was involved and even suspected as a murderer. K has written a novel based on Mr. Arai's notes, which, according to Mr. Shigeto, Mr. Arai himself handed to K, expecting K

to analyze his inner thoughts. Although the police have concluded
that the high school teacher killed his ex-girl friend on the sea and
drowned himself after the murder, and Mr. Arai, who had been
engaged with her and was on the boat with them, was sleeping in the
cabin and had nothing to do with the murder, K has made up a story in
which a young man kills a woman in a park after or while raping her,
but another man in his fifties comes by, assaults the dead woman
again, takes on himself the role of the murderer, and eventually kills
himself. After telling Ma-chan about the connection between the
murder case and K's novel, and suggesting that the story seems a "an
image of Christ's crucifixion weirdly distorted" イエス・キリストの磔
刑の、奇怪な裏がえし (267), Mrs. Shigeto adds that the novel is
motivated by K's own "strange desire to perform this man's sacrifice"
この男の犠牲を演じたいという不思議な欲求, though "in real life, . . .
instead of sacrificing himself, he has a tendency to sacrifice others for
him" 実際の生活では、・・・自分が犠牲になるどころか、他の人を自
分の犠牲にする傾向さえある (267). At Mr. Shigeto's advice,
Ma-chan reads her father's novel and quotes in her "Diary as Home,"
which she is keeping during her parents' absence, a passage:

> 僕が子供の時分のある日、のちに考えれば死ぬ直前の
> 父親がこういったことがある。――おまえのために、
> 他の人間が命を棄ててくれるはずはない、そういうこ
> とがありうると思ってはならない。おまえが頭の良い
> 子供だとチヤホヤされるうちに、誰かおまえよりほか
> の人間で、その人自身の命よりおまえの命が価値があ
> ると、そのように考えてくれる者が出てくるなどと、
> 思ってはならない。それは人間のもっとも悪い堕落だ。
> (268)

One day when I was a child, a day that turned out later to be
just before he died, my father told me: Don't expect
someone to die for you. That never happens. If you have
been told by people around you how clever you are, and you

have been thinking that there will be someone who thinks
his or her life is less worthy than yours, you're wrong. That
is the worst human depravity.

This passage appears in Oe's short story, "Oyogu otoko—mizu no
naka no 'ame no ki'" (The Swimming Man—the "Rain Tree" in the
Water), included in *"Ame no ki" o kiku onna tachi* (Women Who
Listen to the "Rain Tree"), and the story described here in Ma-chan's
narrative exactly matches with the short story. The short story is
narrated by "I," Oe's recurrent and habitual first-person male narrator.
As Mrs. Shigeto suggests, the short story is not so much concerned
with Mr. Arai (appears as Mr. Tamari) as "I"'s, or K's, "strange desire
to act out this man's sacrifice," or even his split desire to act out both
the murder and the sacrifice. In other words, K wrote the novel (short
story) not about Mr. Arai, but "I," his double. Now quoting the above
passage from her father's novel, Ma-chan, who is narrating her
narrative as "I," looks like another K: Ma-chan is now her father's
double.

In her narrative, Ma-chan is repeating what her father has done in
his novel; Ma-chan is asking herself whether she can sacrifice herself
for others, or whether she would rather have others sacrifice
themselves for her. The answer is rather simple. When Mr. Arai tries
to assault her, she runs away, leaving Eeyore as he is fighting Mr. Arai
for her. Now Ma-chan does what her father has done by leaving
Eeyore in Tokyo and going to California to save the "pinch."
Speaking of the subject-object relationship, Ma-chan is no longer an
object who is sacrificed by her father or Eeyore; rather, like her father,
she is the subject who is sacrificing Eeyore. Ma-chan fails to narrate
her narrative on her own; Ma-chan is narrating through the same "I"
as her father has used. Ma-chan's "I" is K's or even Oe's "I."

Here, again, however, Ma-chan inserts a space in her/father's
narrative. She recalls the scenes that follow immediately after she fled
out of Mr. Arai's apartment:

やって来た通りを戻るつもりで駆けて行った道が、逆
方向の、片側に婦人会館や老人福祉会館の敷地のある
一郭で、救いをもとめようにも通行人はいず、灯のつ
いた民家もなかったこと。ハーハーと息を荒くして砂
利とセメントの頑丈な板を並べた昇り坂を駆けるうち、
転んでしまい、いつかの女の子のように膝で歩いて逃
げたこと、ウーウーと泣きもしたこと。やっと立上っ
て歩きだしたものの、自分が兄を肋骨を蹴りつけて折
るような新井君の手におとしたまま逃げたという思い
にとらえられたこと。イーヨーは両親に見棄てられ、
私にも見棄てられた、本当の「すてご」なのに、勇敢
に私を救けようとしていると、あらためて大声をたて
て泣いたこと (279)

That I thought I was running in the direction that I had come,
but it turned out to be the opposite, and there were neither
passersby to ask for help, nor houses with lights on—
nothing except Women's Center and Elderly Citizens' Welfare Center. That I climbed up the slope of pebbles and hard
cemented slabs, panting, and fell, but kept trying to get
away on my knees, like the girl I had seen the other day, and
also cried. That I finally stood up and began to walk, but
suddenly was caught by the idea that I had run away on my
own, leaving my brother in the hands of Mr. Arai, who
could kick and break his ribs. That I began to cry out loud,
thinking of Eeyore, who was truly an abandoned child,
forsaken by both parents and even by me now, yet was
trying to save me, bravely.

In the original, every sentence in this paragraph ends with *koto* こと.
In English, the equivalent is a that-clause. This paragraph seems to be
out of place; it disrupts the current of the narrative. Because of those
"that"s, it seems to be stressed that these sentences belong to the
present of narration, not to that of the events narrated. As a whole, the

paragraph becomes a quotation; it is quoted by Ma-chan from Father's language. By narrating a quotation, Ma-chan reveals herself as an operation within Father's language. The paragraph allows the reader to glimpse such an operation—which Derrida calls writing and Irigaray femininity—lurking in Ma-chan's narration. Now it seems as if every sentence in the narrative is quoted by Ma-chan. True, it is narrated in Father's language. But if it is not quoted by Ma-chan, nobody can read it. True, Father's language makes Ma-chan's narrative possible. But it is also true that Ma-chan's narration makes her father's language possible. Then, we should ask who is quoting and who is quoted, or who is narrating in whose language, or who is the subject and who is the object. Although Oe seems to hate deconstruction, or at least think it obsolete in his conversation with Said held in 1995, what Oe is doing here—at the time when he wrote *A Quiet Life*—seems deconstructive.[22]

Ma-chan of *A Quiet Life* cannot blame her father for having abandoned his children, because she has done the same to her brother Eeyore. Precisely because she does the same as her father does, however, she can criticize her father. She is his critical double. As another "I," Ma-chan narrates the story of her failure to help Eeyore. By narrating the story of her failure, Ma-chan criticizes "I"'s—both hers and her father's—authoritarian presence over Eeyore. Ma-chan's long-standing doubt is that as daughter-sister she has been sacrificed for her family, especially for K and Eeyore. Now she finds out, however, that as an "I," the subject, she has been objectifying Eeyore as her father does. At the very end of the novel, her mother advises Ma-chan to change the title of her diary, "Diary as Home," because it sounds "plain and dull" 愛想もこそもない (285). "Diary as Home" is the means for Ma-chan to center her subjective eyes in the family, and in this sense, it corresponds to K's "I" novels, with which he, Father, represents the family. At her mother's advice, however, Ma-chan gives up the title which sounds as if she represented the whole family. Instead of renaming it herself, Ma-chan asks Eeyore to do so. Eeyore ironically suggests that it should be called "A Quiet

Life," because "That's what our life is" それは私たちの生活のことで
すからね (285). Here, we can hear Eeyore's criticism against both K's
and Ma-chan's race for hegemony in the family and their common
ambition to represent "our life" and keep it "quiet."

As we have seen in the introduction to this chapter, Oe
experiences a feminist turn in the 1980s. Oe's aim is to cause a
critical difference between Japan and his own Yoknapatawpha-
like microcosm. Especially, later in the decade, Oe's feminist turn is
focused on the revision of "I," his recurrent first-person male narrator,
since the first-person male narration is the key agent of Japanese
male-centered ways of thinking. *An Echo of Heaven* and *A Quiet Life*
are the fruits of such a revision of the male "I." In *An Echo of Heaven*,
Oe criticizes "I" through the female character; in *A Quiet Life*, Oe
becomes the female "I." Marie in *An Echo of Heaven* slips out of the
grips of the first-person male narrator "I"; Ma-chan in *A Quiet Life*
lurks in her father's language and deconstructs the male "I"'s authority. What Oe is doing is, as Derrida says of Nietzsche, to "suspend
truth between the tenter-hooks of quotation marks," that is, to suspend
his habitual male "I" in quotation marks.

As we have seen above, *The Town*, *The Mansion*, and *Requiem for
a Nun*, among others, can be read as models to understand Oe's
feminist revision of "I" effectuated through *An Echo of Heaven* and *A
Quiet Life*. As a matter of fact, to a certain extent, at least, Oe's
feminist turn in the 1980s is the result of his reading Faulkner,
especially the later novels. Oe's revision of "I" in the 1980s results in
the 1990s in the androgynous narrator of the Flaming Green Tree
trilogy and the homosexual focal character of *Somersault*. There, as
we will see in the following chapter, we see another Faulknerian
connection. For Oe, the revision of "I" perfected through *An Echo of
Heaven* and *A Quiet Life* marks an important step in developing his
own Yoknapatawpha. After *An Echo of Heaven* and *A Quiet Life*, Oe's
"I" is no longer an authoritarian, central eye in the microcosm built
on his native village. It forms a clear contrast with the Emperor's gaze
or the eyes of the authoritarian male which is still at the center of

Japanese culture. In the Flaming Green Tree trilogy and *Somersault*, Oe's fictional native village in Shikoku is again Japan's critical double. After *An Echo of Heaven* and *A Quiet Life*, however, it becomes even more critical of the authoritarian Japan, especially of its sense of time, which, presided over by the Emperor's "I" or eye, supports the illusion of Japan's immortality. As we will see in the following chapter, the androgynous "I" or the homosexual focal character in the Flaming Green Tree trilogy and *Somersault* urges us to see through such an illusion.

Notes

1. Although I am indebted to Butler for the concept of "gender trouble" that includes a deconstruction of the binary relationship between the male subject and the female object, Butler herself seems to be more interested in Foucaultdian analysis of power that stabilizes such a relationship. See Butler xxvii–xxviii.

2. In Deborah Clarke's *Robbing the Mother: Women in Faulkner*, which was not available to Oe in 1981, we can find a comprehensive expression of what has been pointed out by Bleikastan, Brooks, and Williams. Referring mainly to Kristeva, Clarke traces how Faulkner's female characters, while appearing as "mother as absent center," gain a "creative power" (18).

3. Tsushima Yuko and Oe Kenzaburo, 「想像力と女性的なもの」 ("Imagination and the Feminine"), *Sekai* (Aug. 1985): 136–52; Tomioka Taeko and Oe Kenzaburo, 「言葉そして文学へ」 ("From Language to Literature"), *Gunzo* (Aug. 1985): 136–62.

4. In the postscript entitled "Ma-chan" attached to the 1995 pocket-book edition of *Shizukana seikatu*, Oe writes: "Creating this narrator [Ma-chan] led me to read Yeats more, and also discover the androgynous narrator, Satchan, of *Moeagaru midori no ki*, which I wrote on that experience of reading Yeats, and which, so far, would be my last novels" (my translation); この語り手を作り出しえたことが、私がイェーツを読むことをさらに進め、その経験に立ちながら書いた、いまのところ「最後の小説」で

ある長編『燃えあがる緑の木』の、両性具有の人物サッチャンという
語り手、語り方を発見させることにもなったのでした (290).

5. For a discussion of the Name-of-the-Father, see Dor (83–134).

6. The original argument by Jung is found in Jung and Kerényi (86–98).

7. Noel Polk has already made the point: "Stevens and Nancy, live, then, at polarized extremes; their worlds are very nearly mutually exclusive, and yet both, from their limited experiences of life, idealistically attempt to "save" Temple, a character who stands morally, socially, and psychologically between the two extremes they represent: she knows both worlds, both sides of her own nature, and has been trying for years to live with the incredible guilt and anguish her experiences [recounted in *Sanctuary*] have caused her. She is therefore much more complex, her burden much greater, than either Stevens or Nancy can ever understand. She has none of the answers, none of the certainties, that they seem to have, and none of their calm spiritual repose in the face of the world's overwhelming questions" (*Faulkner's Requiem for a Nun* 62).

8. Using Lacan and Žižek, Evelyn Jaffe Schreiber describes the mechanism, in which Gavin, or men of Jefferson, establishes his or their subjectivity through the distance to Eula or Linda. Schreiber writes, for example: "In the Snopes trilogy, Eula Varner and Linda Snopes Kohl become the *object petit a* of Yoknapatawpha County, sustaining the community's identity by always being out of reach. Because the object is purely imaginary and nor real, it has a power that drives individuals not to attain the object but to keep it perpetually unattainable" (87).

9. For a discussion of Gavin's romanticism, see Brooks, *William Faulkner: The Yoknapatawpha Country* (192–218).

10. Brooks writes: "Yet, a few hours after telling this to Gavin, Eula will commit suicide to protect the good name of her daughter. The point is that Eula does not see herself as dying for honor—not at least in the man's sense of the term. Her act is practical; it shows a concern with facts, or at least with the way in which facts fit together. Her suicide is based on what Eula regards as the realities of human nature and particularly of feminine nature. / Eula is apparently not interested in respectability—only in a special and limited way.

She doubtless is aware that most of the town knows about her relationship with Manfred de Spain. She may even suspect that a great many people think that Flem Snopes is not actually the father of her child. Even so, Linda still has a name and social position which are not jeopardized by people's knowing these things. On the other hand, Linda will clearly suffer if the fact of her mother's adultery is proclaimed and the public forced to take cognizance of it" (*William Faulkner: The Yoknapatawpha Country* 209–10). In a session at the University of Virginia, Faulkner himself says: "the mother felt that it would be better for this girl to have a mother who committed suicide than a mother who ran off with a lover" (Gwynn and Blotner 195).

11. Drawing on Luce Irigaray, Dawn Trouard has already made a similar point: "Eula *embodies* the 'economic of fluids,' the first of the Irigarayian principles demonstrated in the trilogy. She is both challenge and alternative to the patriarchal economics that pervade the hamlet and town, communities governed by the economic order of 'solids' (idealism, phallocentrism, hierarchy). This is the system that Flem Snopes desires, invades, and masters" (281).

12. Keith Louise Fulton stresses Faulkner's intention to oppose patriarchy through the figure of Linda: "How did Faulkner come up with the character of Linda? Perhaps he was aware of the other 'civil war' being fought by women, a civil war against the authority of the fathers" (435).

13. All references to the original *Jinsei no shinseki* in this study are to Oe Kenzaburo, *Jinsei no shinseki* (Tokyo: Shinchosha, 1994). For the translation, I used Margaret Mitsutani's—Oe Kenzaburo, *An Echo of Heaven* (Tokyo: Kodansha International, 2000)—, unless otherwise noted.

14. For example, the publisher's ad on the jacket of the pocket book edition of *Jinsei no shinseki*, which I am using in the present study, seems to be misleading.

15. In the original Japanese, Marie's letter is not italicized, and therefore hard to be distinguished from "I"'s sentences.

16. Flannery O'Connor's first name is Mary. For her pseudonym, O'Connor dropped it "to resist the feminizing and softening associated with the southern tradition of double names for girls" (Gordon 24).

17. It is not certain whether Temple has intended to take the six-month-old baby with her or leave her. Nancy refers to both. But it does not matter what Temple has intended. It is when Temple says to Nancy, "Yes! Children or no children," that she abandons, *de facto*, both her children.

18. This seems to be what Faulkner meant, when he spoke of Nancy's "environment" in *Faulkner in the University*. See Gwynn and Blotner 196.

19. See, for example, Althusser 31.

20. Janet Wondra has already focused on the ideological function of language in *Requiem for a Nun*, mainly drawing on Bakhtin's conception of "play": "Every utterance participates in the 'unitary language' (in its centripetal forces and tendencies) and at the same time partakes of social and historical heteroglossia (the centrifugal, stratifying forces)" (qtd. in Wondra 46). Wondra asserts: "Just as Faulkner's narrative voice is constructed within a language saturated by the ideology of white male privilege, so the dramatic voices of Nancy and Temple must speak through saturated language, but avoid sounding like the voice of a male god speaking through female oracles" (56). While I agree with Wondra in most parts, my emphasis is more on the failed conversation between Temple and Nancy rather than on "many emotions shared by Temple and Nancy" (Wondra 58).

21. All references to the original *Shizukana seikatsu* in this study are to Oe Kenzaburo, *Shizukana seikatsu* (Tokyo: Kodansha, 1995). All translations are mine.

22. In his conversation with Said, Oe expresses his sympathy with Said, whom he calls "the first to say that the role of deconstruction is now over" (my translation); ディコンストラクション（脱構築）の役割は終わったということをいちばん最初に言った人 (Oe and Said 27).

Chapter Three

The "Problems of the Spirit" / the "Matters of the Soul"

The Radical Spirit/Soul and the End of the World

As a metaphor for "*is*," Yoknapatawpha is opposed to the idea of immortality as such. "*Is*" exists in each individual, not in the mass, in the nation, or in the human race as a whole. If Oe's Yoknapatawpha is a metaphor for such an "*is*," it has to be distinguished from Japan, its metaphorical counterpart, which has nourished its own idea of immortality around the immortal presence of the Emperor. Oe's criticism is directed toward such an idea of immortality. We will see in what follows a curious parallel between Oe and Faulkner. In *A Fable*, Faulkner also sets himself to distinguish his idea of "*is*" from its seeming counterpart, *man*'s immortality. Moreover, Faulkner and Oe share the idea that a pursuit of immortality paradoxically brings about its flip side, *i.e.*, the end of the world.

In his Nobel Prize speech, Faulkner criticizes his era for its lack of attention to the "problems of the spirit": "There are no longer problems of the spirit. There is only the question: When will I be blown up?" ("Upon Receiving" 119) It seems that Faulkner is feigning an anachronism, the same anachronism he purposely uses in *A Fable*, the novel which he was writing then. In *A Fable*, Christ appears at the battle front of World War I; in the Nobel Prize speech, Faulkner calls attention to the spirit in an age which disrespects the "problems of the spirit."[1] If, as Urgo argues, *A Fable* is a novel concerned with the rebellious, anti-authoritarian spirit (*Faulkner's Apocrypha* 105–22), we can see its connection to the "spirit" mentioned in his Nobel Prize speech: in both the speech and the novel, the spirit is set against Authority, which appears not only as the institution or technocracy which supports modern wars, but also as the idea of total human extinction as the inevitable consequence of the advancement of genocidal technology. In fact, what is common to the novel and the speech is the image of the totally devastated world, especially, in view of the time—the early 1950s—when they are published, the apocalyptic image of thermonuclear annihilation: in *A Fable*, the Old General suggests to the Corporal, concerning a devastated world, that "last ding dong of doom had rung and died" (299); in the speech, Faulkner uses the same phrase to describe the end of the world: the "last ding-dong of doom has clanged and faded from the last worthless rock hanging tideless in the last red and dying evening" (120).[2]

In his Nobel Prize acceptance speech in 1994, forty-four years after Faulkner's, Oe also feigns an anachronism by expressing his support for the ninth article of the Japanese Constitution, which prohibits the government from waging war as a means to solve the international conflicts:

> In recent years there have been criticisms leveled against Japan suggesting that it should offer more military support to the United Nations forces and thereby play a more active role in the keeping and restoration of peace in various parts of the world. Our hearts sink whenever we hear these comments. After the Second World War it was a categorical

> imperative for Japan to renounce war forever as a central
> article of the new constitution. The Japanese chose, after
> their painful experiences, the principle of permanent peace
> as the moral basis for their rebirth. ("Japan, the Ambiguous,
> and Myself" 119)

Article 9 of the Japanese Constitution has already been contradicting the U.S.-Japan Security Treaty and, in this sense, it is not only anachronistic but also naïve to keep advocating it at its face value. However, once we notice that Oe's anachronism or naiveté expressed in the Nobel Prize speech is linked to the "matters [or deeds] of the soul" described in the novels on which Oe was working then—*Moeagaru midori no ki: sanbusaku* (A Flaming Green Tree: Trilogy), we can understand that it is not feigned but, on the contrary, seriously maintained. In the speech, Oe reveals his debt to Yeats, for whom he feels "spiritual affinity," for the title of the trilogy, which is taken from a stanza in Yeats' poem, "Vacillation" (114). Oe also quotes a passage not by Yeats, but from the motion read at the Irish Senate in celebrating Yeats' winning the Nobel Prize in 1923, a passage which conveys a fear sensed during World War I, a war which had almost devastated the western civilization:

> Our civilization will be assessed on the name of Senator
> Yeats. Coming at a time when there was a regular wave of
> destruction [and] hatred of beauty . . . it is a very happy and
> welcome thing. . . . [T]here will always be the danger that
> there may be a stampeding of people who are sufficiently
> removed from insanity in enthusiasm for destruction. (qtd.
> in Oe, "Japan, the Ambiguous, and Myself" 115–16)

Faulkner's Christ, the corporal Stefan, appears at the front of World War I, but, as suggested in the old general's words above, the novel is implicitly concerned with the situation in which Faulkner was writing it, that is, the incipient stage of the Cold War, or the age after

Hiroshima and Nagasaki, that is, the nuclear age. In creating the corporal in the midst of the Cold War, Faulkner imagines a protagonist who is seen trying to stop a battle on the Western front during World War I, but who can also be read as opposing the race of nuclear weapons.[3] Similarly, in Oe's Flaming Green Tree trilogy, a religious movement originated from Brother Gii's personal wish to devote himself to the "matters of the soul" develops into a protest movement against the atomic power generation. For Oe, the "matters of the soul" and the idea of permanent peace declared in Article 9 of the Japanese Constitution coincide and are together opposed to the nuclear forces, that are indiscriminately represented by the nuclear weapons and the atomic power plants.

In his Nobel Prize speech, Oe points out a tendency in Japan to promulgate the vision of a dark future, in which Japan resumes its militarism on the pretext of contributing to the world order, and consequently takes part in the global nuclearism:

> In Japan itself there have all along been attempts by some people to remove the article about renunciation of war from the constitution, and for this purpose they have taken every opportunity to make use of pressure from abroad. But to remove the principle of permanent peace would be an act of betrayal toward the people of Asia and the victims of the bombs dropped on Hiroshima and Nagasaki. It is not difficult for me as a writer to imagine the outcome. (120)

We can see here a similar, purposely anachronistic appeal to the "problems of the spirit" to which Faulkner called attention in his Nobel Prize speech. For Oe, to stick to the idea of permanent peace corresponds to what Faulkner calls the "problems of the spirit." For both Faulkner and Oe, the spirit/soul is meant to be an objection to the global nuclearism.

Before we hasten to see a parallel between Faulkner and Oe, however, we have to consider a possible gap between the two writers in the understanding of the meaning of peace, since Oe's support for the idea of permanent peace apparently contradicts the rejection of pacifism that Faulkner expressed in his prefatory note to *A Fable*. In the note, which was rejected by the publisher, Faulkner insisted on the use of "fire" to fight fire ("A Note" 416). By suggesting the use of "fire" to fight fire, however, Faulkner does not mean to encourage warfare between countries. Rather, Faulkner encourages us—the reader, people, civilians—to fight governments, the authorities, that declare wars. Referring to the portion of the note which follows the above, Urgo asserts that Faulkner "disavows any faith in 'nations or governments or ideologies' as defenders against war or as tools through which wars might finally end," and "implores 'simple human beings vulnerable to death and injury,' the ones who 'will be the first to be destroyed,' to become conscious of their power to confront and overrun the warmakers" (*Faulkner's Apocrypha* 101). Then, we should say that Faulkner is not opposing pacifism, but radicalizing it.

In *A Fable*, as we will see later, radical pacifism takes various forms. The corporal's is one of them. There are others, and among them is one representing an extremely radical pacifism which looks almost the opposite of the corporal's pacifism: that is, the radicalism represented by the English battalion runner.[4] Influenced by the corporal's mutiny, but perhaps more by the story of the horse theft and the sentry's Masonry heard from Sutterfield, the runner leads the second mutiny, and brings a whole battalion to total destruction.[5] As Urgo points out, it is in the runner's radicalization that the corporal's rebellious spirit is linked to the spirit of the horse which runs on three legs (*Faulkner's Apocrypha* 114–16). However, in the runner's radical synthesis of the two different spirits, each of them is deformed. The crucial difference that separates the runner from the corporal or the horse is that the runner never dies. After a temporary success, the corporal's mutiny is soon suppressed, and the corporal is executed; similarly, after the last glorious days, the three-legged horse is probably killed by its groom, that is, the sentry, who joins the Masons during those glorious fifteen days. When Sutterfield tells the runner that what he, his grandson, and the sentry went through was "an apotheosis" (Faulkner, *A Fable* 129), he sounds as if he is speaking not only of the horse but also of the corporal. Sutterfield suggest that the story he is now telling is immortal, while the incident, or the person who causes it, passes through the story. Like other examples which we have seen through the previous two chapters, we can see here another echo of Faulkner's words in his interview with Jean Stein: "time is a fluid condition which has no existence except in the momentary avatars of individual people." The corporal is mortal; so is the horse. Only their stories are immortal.

On the contrary, the runner finds himself immortal. Although he says after the second mutiny, "They cant kill us! They cant! Not dare not: they cant!" (272), he is the only survivor of the mutiny which he himself has caused. At the end of the novel, after throwing the medal against the old general's casket and himself being thrown by the crowd into a gutter, the runner also says, "I'm not going to die. Never" (370). Of course, as Brooks ironizes, he is going to die someday: "Men die. Ideas do not, and what speaks here is an idea, an idea very thinly clothed in human flesh and blood" (*William Faulkner: Toward Yoknapatawpha* 250). At the end of the novel, however, he is described as "not a man but a mobile and upright scar, on crutches," with "one arm and one leg" (368). The runner is the corporal deformed; the runner's physical damages represent the damages done to the corporal's spirit. When he says that he is not going to die, he is implicitly comparing himself with the corporal who has successfully died a martyr to his resistant spirit. The runner has led other soldiers to death, but he himself has become a symbol of immortality, which is not so much "very thinly clothed in human flesh and blood" as inhumanly deformed. Moreover, in the figure of the runner is implied his physical resemblance—though deformed—to the horse; the runner is walking on three legs, that is, on one leg and two crutches.

Radicalization is also an important motif in Oe's Flaming Green Tree trilogy. In *Oinaru hi ni* (On the Day of Glory), the third novel in the trilogy, Brother Gii decides to separate himself from the religious movement which he himself started and has allowed to connect to the anti-nuclear movement, saying, "I think it is most desirable that each of us engage in the matters of the soul separately" (my translation) or バラバラになった者たちが、それぞれに魂のことをやるというのが、一番望ましいと思うんだよ (350). In the trilogy, radicalization is represented by the centripetal tendency in the religious movement of the Church of the "Flaming Green Tree," propelled by the Ino brothers—Ai, Iku, and Ei—who have followed Brother Gii since the early stage of the movement. It is they who set the destination of the "march of the world missions" 世界伝道の行進 at a nuclear power plant. In Brother Gii's original idea, its purpose was "only for the church members to go out of the woods and march outward" (my translation) 教会員たちが森のなかの土地から外に出て行進する (209). Contrary to Brother Gii's centrifugal and individualistic tendency, however, the Ino brothers insist on unifying and organizing the church in preparation for the more aggressive missions.

In *Chugaeri* (*Somersault*), which Oe published in 1999 as a kind of sequel to the trilogy, the motif of radicalization is more clearly presented. In *Somersault*, as Brother Gii separates himself from his own church in the trilogy, two leaders of a religious movement, called Patron and Guide, suddenly, as if making a somersault, renounce the movement itself. The reason is to prevent the radical faction of their church from making a terror raid on nuclear power plants for the purpose of blowing them up and letting the world realize their apocalyptic teaching. In the Flaming Green Tree trilogy, when the church members pray at the same time during the march, two of the reactors at the nuclear power plant coincidentally, yet accidentally, stop working. Although even Brother Gii is inclined to believe in the miraculous effect of their concentrated prayers, there was no intention for the church members, either for Brother Gii or for the Ino brothers, to do more than simply to protest against the nuclear power in general, let alone to blow up the power plant. In *Somersault*, on the other hand, by blowing up the nuclear power plants, the radicals intend to hasten the end of the world with their own hands. In the trilogy, Brother Gii's decision to separate himself from the church does not necessarily oppose the church's, or his own, moderate antinuclearism. In *Somersault*, on the other hand, Patron and Guide's "somersault" is addressed directly to the radicals' antinuclearism, which as a consequence of their radicalization, has ironically become a nuclearism in itself. Just as the runner in *A Fable* leads a whole battalion to destruction and finds himself alone immortal, the radicals in *Somersault* intend to lead the whole human race to destruction and also, though paradoxically, to promulgate their teaching after the end of the world. What is common to both the runner in *A Fable* and the radicals in *Somersault* is the fact that what they do with their good, but radical, intentions—or consciences—can only contribute to hastening the destruction or the end of the world. This sounds like a metaphor for the situation, or the time, itself, in which you have to fight wars to stop wars, or to prevent the nuclear wars, you have to have more nuclear weapons than you can erase the whole human race. In other words, it is a metaphor for the paradox that to seek for the permanence, or immortality, of human world, you have to bring it to an end.

In what follows, I will discuss *A Fable* and *Somersault* in more details. In each novel, one who holds the key to understanding the entire structure of the novel is a hermaphrodite: the old general in *A Fable* and Ikuo in *Somersault*. To me, the runner seems to take sides with the old general, who represents the paradoxical situation described above, but, at the same time, the old general, who is a kind of hermaphrodite, takes sides with the corporal, or what Faulkner calls the spirit.[6] In *Somersault*, Patron repeats what Brother Gii, his precursor, has done by giving priority to his matters of soul over the matters of the church, and his will is inherited by Ikuo, who concludes the novel by saying that their church is the "place where deeds of the soul are done" (570). But Ikuo, who is practically a hermaphrodite, also succeeds to the radicalism of Guide, Patron's partner, who created the radical faction of the church, wishing to end

the world. In both *A Fable* and *Somersault*, hermaphroditism serves
as a metaphor which summarizes the difficulty, or the paradox, a
spirit or a soul has to face in the time when we have to use "fire" to
fight fire. For Oe, as I have suggested in Introduction, such a paradox
reflects the situation of Japan, which was led by the Emperor's or the
authoritarian male's sense of immortality to the devastating Second
World War. In our reading, *A Fable* will be read as a guide to
understanding Oe's criticism of Japan's patriarchy, especially of its
belief in immortality which, if sought for as such, only turns into its
flip side, the end of the world.

Hermaphroditism of War: *A Fable*

In their confrontation, the old general tells the corporal of the
hermaphroditism of war:

> the phenomenon of war is its hermaphroditism: the princi-
> ples of victory and defeat inhabit the same body and the
> necessary opponent, enemy, is merely the bed they self-
> exhaust each other on: a vice only the more terrible and
> fatal because there is no intervening breast or division
> between to frustrate them into health by simple normal
> distance and lack of opportunity for the copulation from
> which even orgasm cannot free them. (Faulkner, *A Fable*
> 291)

Autoerotic or even homosexual activities, implied here, are a metaphor for war or the "principles of victory and defeat." In *A Fable*,
men join the military, or war, trying to escape from the feminine,
"intervening breast," or intersexual "copulation," which is regarded as
"health[ier]," but, at the same time, "frustrat[ing]." The feminine and
intersexual relationships are the metaphor for peace, or the normal
life, to which men prefer war, or death. At war, men indulge in
autoerotic or homosexual activities of victory and defeat.

Here, however, Faulkner allows his metaphors to restore their literal meanings also. Men find in the military, or war, the equivalents for those from which they believe they have escaped: that is, they imaginatively, not necessarily actually, replace the intersexual activities in the ordinary life with the autoerotic or homosexual activities in the military and cause a "gender trouble." That is why, as both Polk and Godden illustrate, hermaphroditic, homoerotic and even scatological images haunt Levine, Gragnon, the runner, the horse, the old general, and the corporal.[7] In *A Fable*, not only victory and defeat, but also male and female, anus and vagina, sky and earth, foods and excrements, war and peace commingle.

When the old general tells the corporal of the "hermaphroditism" of war, he also hints at the hermaphroditism of their relationship, the relationship in which he and the corporal are not enemies but rather two similar hermaphrodites. The old general tells the corporal of his dark vision of the future, in which man is enslaved to the advanced technologies of war, but "outlast[s] even his wars" by "inculcating their masters with the slaves' own vices—in this case the vice of war and that other one which is no vice at all but instead is the quality-mark and warrant of man's immortality: his deathless folly" (298).[8] The old general is sarcastic. Among the characters in *A Fable*, he is the most cynical, pessimistic, radical ironist. For him, man's immortality lies in his being hand in hand with his folly. Man not only survives his "frankenstein" (299)—the deadly weapons, such as the nuclear weapon which "permits him the harmless delusion that he controls it from the ground with buttons"—by "inculcating" it with the "vice of war," which the old general also calls the "hermaphroditism" of war, or the "principles of victory and of defeat inhabit-[ing] the same body." He also "prevail[s]," that is, "after the last ding dong of doom had rung and died there will be one sound more: his voice, planning still to build something higher and faster and louder; more efficient and louder and faster than ever before, yet it too inherent with the same old primordial fault since it too in the end will fail to eradicate him from the earth" (299). To endure and prevail, therefore, means a repetition, a vicious circle, in which men try to kill each other, and women as well, with more and more deadly weapons, and yet keep failing forever. In other words, in his immortality, man endures a devastation, prevails in the more devastating technology, endures another devastation, and so forth on. The old general thus envisions man's immortality, in which endurance and prevalence commingle and keep circling forever and ever, like two deathless hermaphrodites.

While the old general advocates immortality, the corporal represents death. The old general says that for the corporal, who wants to die a martyr, death is the "actual ace of trumps" (295). To convince the corporal of the value of "simple breathing, simply being alive," or "merely knowing that you are alive" (296), the old general tells the story of a murderer in Mississippi, who had waited for his execution, the moment when he could "doff the sorry ephemeral world," but, at the moment of execution, saw a bird, "one weightless and ephemeral creature" (297), fly onto a bough, and then suddenly began to beg for more life, crying, "Innocent! Innocent! I didn't do it!"

By telling the story of the murderer and the bird, the old general seems to be suggesting that the corporal, or the murderer, should take the bird, that is, a life which is opposed to death, or is supposed to be associated with the old general's idea of immortality. But that is only his pretence. Intentionally, the old general allows the story to work in the opposite way and deconstruct the apparent identification of the old general with the bird, and the corporal with the murderer. In this way, the corporal becomes the bird and the old general the murderer. While advocating man's immortality, the old general knows the value or even beauty of the bird's or life's ephemerality, that is, mortality. At the moment of execution, the murderer realizes that the "earth's grief and anguish," which signifies mortality, is preferable to the "eternal peace," or the immortality, for which he has longed. Although the old general serves man's immortality, he knows that he himself is nothing but a mortal "ephemeral creature." He is well aware that man's immortality eventually comes to a mere repetition, and is, *de facto*, the same as the end of man.[9]

What the old general calls man's immortality resembles what Gavin in *The Town* calls *was*. As I have pointed out in the previous chapter, for Gavin, fixing Eula and Linda as *was* is his means to keep a distance from them. Gavin also identifies *was* with the idea of "Remaining." For Gavin, "Remaining" ultimately means a patriarchal succession, and he sees its illustration in the Snopeses. The old general's "hermaphroditism" of war apparently resembles what Gavin calls the "hermaphroditic principle" of the Snopeses. They both designate man's immortality. In Gavin's male "Remaining," women— say Eula and Linda—are mortal and "doomed to fade; by the fact of that mortality doomed not to assuage nor even negate [man's] hunger" (*The Town* 133). For Gavin, as well as for the old general, man is immortal, whereas woman is mortal and ephemeral.

Now we can understand the gender implications in the story of the murderer in Mississippi and the bird. The murderer, or the old general, means man, and the bird, the corporal, means woman. However, we should at the same time consider the difference between the old general and Gavin. On the one hand, in his poet's task of fixing Eula and Linda in *was*, Gavin always identifies himself with man; on the other hand, telling the corporal of the story of the murderer, who at the last moment of his life is struck by the ephemerality of the bird, the old general reveals his affinity for the feminine mortality. The story, which is supposed to convince the corporal of the value of life, now turns out to be the old general's expression of his sympathy, or pity, for the corporal, which resembles Eula's pity, or sense of AWARE, not only for Gavin alone but also for every human being including herself. In *The Town*, Eula expresses such a pity or sense of AWARE, which means the affection for mortality or ephemerality, as "You just are, and you need, and you must, and so you do" (94). In *A Fable*, especially in his relationship with the old general, the corporal represents such a mortality or ephemerality, and even the sense of AWARE for it. The old general is not "inimical" to such a feminine mortality or ephemerality as represented by the corporal. Rather, the masculine immortality, to which the old general has dedicated his life, or, in other words, his life has been bound, is, as Eula says, a "nuisance" (93) to him.

What the old general calls man's immortality is the negative of what Faulkner in the Jean Stein interview describes as "time [as] a fluid condition which has no existence except in the momentary avatars of individual people." In other words, the old general's idea of man's immortality is a misconception, or a turnover, of Faulkner's fluid time. On the one hand, man's immortality forces every human being to work for it, and involves every human being in a repetition, a vicious circle, which amounts to the idea of the end of man; on the other hand, the fluid time "has no existence" in itself, but appears through momentary freedom of each person, and continues on. Another Faulknerian term for such a fluid time as embodied in each person is "spirit." When Faulkner spoke of the "spirit" in the Nobel Prize speech, referring to *A Fable* on which he was working then, he perhaps had already had in mind the idea of the "time [as] a fluid condition," which he would express later in the 1956 Stein interview. In fact, in the Nobel Prize speech, Faulkner mentions "spirit" in the context in which he opposes the positive picture of immortality, that is, the fluid time, against the old general's idea of man's immortality:

> I decline to accept the end of man. It is easy enough to say that man is immortal simply because he will endure: that when the last ding-dong of doom has clanged and faded from the last worthless rock hanging tideless in the last red and dying evening, that even then there will still be one more sound: that of his puny inexhaustible voice, still talking. I refuse to accept this. I believe that man will not merely endure: he will prevail. He is immortal, not because he alone among creatures has an inexhaustible voice, but because he has a soul, a spirit capable of compassion and sacrifice and endurance. The poet's, the writer's, duty is to write about these things. ("Upon Receiving" 120)

The old general thinks that man is immortal because he has his voice, that is, the will to "build something higher and faster and louder; more efficient and louder and faster than ever before," whereas Faulkner thinks that the human being is immortal because he/she has a "soul, a spirit capable of compassion and sacrifice and endurance." As we have seen, the corporal in *A Fable*—Christ, who anachronistically appears at the front of World War I—is the "spirit" in the age when our minds are preoccupied with the question, "when will I be blown up?" In the present context, the corporal is another Eula, who has a "soul, a spirit capable of compassion and sacrifice and endurance," and chooses death. He conveys to us the sense of being mortal, or being a "momentary avatar" of the fluid time.

We should note here that the old general does not necessarily believe in the idea of man's immortality which he himself advocates. Rather, he is more inclined to take sides with the corporal's mortality. If so, by a "soul, a spirit capable of compassion and sacrifice and endurance," Faulkner is describing not only what the corporal represents but also the old general himself. Obviously, by the time when he made the Nobel Prize speech, Faulkner had already written the conversation scene between the old general and the corporal. There is nothing mysterious about what Faulkner calls a "soul, a spirit." In the speech, Faulkner paraphrases it as the "human heart in conflict with itself which alone can make good writing" (119). By confronting the corporal, his own son, who is willing to die martyr to his ideal, and by ironically telling his son about his dark vision of the future in which man's voice keeps on calling for "something higher and faster and louder," the old general reveals his own "heart in conflict with itself." The old general has a clairvoyant knowledge, but, among other things, he knows his own heart's conflict. On his way to the old Roman citadel accompanied by the corporal, the old general criticizes himself for what he is doing. The old general knows that by meeting the corporal or giving his son his recognition of the meaning of the execution or even willingly acting the role of denying his son's justness, he is going to make the corporal a martyr. The old general tells the corporal that they are together enacting a "paradox" (Faulkner, *A Fable* 295). Even here, the old general is sarcastic; he knows that he is overestimating their dependence on each other: "if I can do without you, then so can you yourself" (295). By setting up the meeting, however, the old general has already been enacting the paradox. He knows that he has already been taking sides with the corporal; he also knows that the corporal will not take what he offers him to take—"car" (291), "freedom" (293), the "earth" (293), the "world" (294), "life" (295), the "bird" (297)—but will rather choose death. With all this knowledge, the old general still has to kill the corporal, because he knows that that is his role to play.

The old general thinks that his job is to serve man's immortality, that is, man and his folly. Although he knows that the corporal would not accept his offer, the old general pretends to offer the job to the corporal. However, what the old general tries to offer to the corporal is not his actual job as the top of the French military hierarchy but what he calls the "heritage" (295). This is a conversation between Satan and Christ. Like the temptation of Jesus in the New Testament, the conversation between the old general and the corporal is carried not metaphorically, but rather literally, if only we accept it as a conversation between Satan and Christ. The old general tells the corporal to inherit Paris from him. Paris here means not Paris but man's immortality itself. The old general knows that the corporal would not take Paris, because he himself has once refused to take it. As he tells the corporal repeatedly, the old general has never "misread" the corporal's character (292, 293), because he was once like the corporal.

The old general leaves Paris after graduating from the Academy, and goes to Africa not as a quartermaster captaincy, which was prepared for him, but as a sublieutenant. After an incident in which he saves a war by sacrificing the life of a soldier who corrupted a Riff woman, the old general goes to Tibet, and there he himself commits fornication with a woman and fathers the corporal, and later discards them to return to Paris.[10] As Fowler points out, these two cases—the case of the soldier who, even before the case of the Riff woman, has "murdered" (Faulkner, *A Fable* 216) a woman in Marseilles, and that of the old general—are the "buried allusions" (Fowler, "'In Another Country'" 47) to the quotation from Christopher Marlow's *The Jew of Malta*, which passes twice in the runner's mind in the chapter entitled "Tuesday Night": "But that was in another country; and besides / the wench is dead" (Faulkner, *A Fable* 59); "—but that was in another country; / and besides, the wench is dead" (69). The runner also has discarded a woman whom he found in London before he enlisted. During the leave after the demotion which he got of his own will, the runner meets the woman and takes his leave of her. In all these three cases, as we have seen above, men join or return to the military to leave women. However, as Fowler says, we do not have to be "too literal-minded" about the allusion to the "dead wenches" ("'In Another Country'" 53). In the military, men indulge in what the old general calls the "hermaphroditism" of war, or the "principles of victory and of defeat inhabit[ing] the same body," which only lead to the vicious circle, the repetition of "man and his folly." In the eyes of the old general who stays in Africa or Tibet, the military life in Paris could be another "wench," or a death, "in another country." As the corporal tried to stop war, the old general has once dumped war, the military, or his "wench." However, he returns to Paris, and devotes himself to his job of serving man's immortality, which he knows paradoxically means the *de facto* end of human beings. In this sense, the old general has left a "wench" "in another country" in two ways. He has dumped both the human, feminine, mortality and man's immortality.

Here is the old general's hermaphroditism in terms of his relationship with the military, and also in terms of the relationship with the runner and the corporal respectively: on the one hand, like the runner, the old general returns to the military after leaving a "wench" in Tibet, "in another country"; on the other hand, like the corporal, the old general has once said no to the military in Paris and war in Africa, that is, "in another country," and escaped to Africa or

Tibet respectively. But, to speak of such a hermaphroditism, the runner and the corporal are both hermaphrodites, too. Indeed, the runner returns to the military, but his decision to be demoted is the sign of his half-way attitude toward the military; moreover, like the corporal, he causes a mutiny. On the other hand, as his half-sister Marthe reveals, and if she is correct, the corporal, who would later try to stop war, joins the military motivated by rather a simple, nationalistic reason. He joins the military to defend France and what France gave him, that is, "that dignity and right and that security and independence" (Faulkner, *A Fable* 253). Moreover, like the runner, the corporal returns to the military, even if to lead a mutiny, after leaving his fiancée, a Marseille whore, whom he has probably met during his service in war. We see here a commingling of three hermaphrodites: the old general, the corporal, and the runner.

In this context, in *A Fable* there is another important pair of elements that commingle: laugher and tears. At the end of the novel, thrown into the gutter, the runner begins to "laugh, or tried to" (370). Then the quartermaster general holds the runner's head and shoulders in his arms, and in the "cradle of the old man's arm," the runner says in French, "Tremble. I'm not going to die. Never" (370). The runner's laughter is not triumphant, but rather self-scorning; he laughs at his being different from the corporal or his being solely and gratuitously immortal. As Polk calls the scene a piéta ("Woman and the Feminine" 202), the runner is another Christ, but a self-styled, deformed one. The quartermaster general sees that the runner is laughing or at least trying to laugh, and, as if he understands the runner's self-depreciation and wants to console him, says: "I am not laughing. . . . What you see are tears" (Faulkner, *A Fable* 370).

Perhaps the quartermaster general knows who the man in his arms is and also understands his grudge against the old general who executed the corporal, his hero. Here, the quartermaster general pretends to be the one who alone understands the conflict between the old general and the corporal, and his tears, which signify pity or sorrow, look like the concluding remark of the novel. However, there is one important thing that the quartermaster general does not know: he does not know, nor does the runner, that the corporal is now lying side by side with the old general, his father. Here is the irony for which all such complicated process depicted in the first third of the final chapter entitled "Tomorrow," in which the corporal's corpse comes back as the corpse of the Unknown Soldier, is made up. Perhaps there is none in the crowd, none except for the old general and the corporal themselves, who understands the irony that has resulted from the process, the irony that after so much psychological conflict the father and the son finally lie dying abreast.[11] What concludes the novel is this irony, or the fact that both the old general and the corporal eventually turn out to be two mortal beings. In this sense, neither the runner's laughter nor the quartermaster general's tears cannot be the novel's last word. Like Levine's suicide, each of them embodies the respective part of what Faulkner calls the "trinity of conscience," but the irony at the end of the novel tells the reader that none of the three has privilege over the other two.[12]

The motif of the "trinity of conscience" seems to be so important for Faulkner; he concludes his prefatory note to *A Fable* by explaining it in connection to the ending of the novel. According to the note, the "trinity of conscience" is represented by three attitudes toward the "world" and the "evil" (Faulkner, "A Note" 417). For Levine, the "world" is "evil," so he has to terminate the whole of it; for the quartermaster general, the "world" and the "evil" are separate, but, for now, it so happens that the "world" looks like the "evil" itself; for the runner, the "world" is not "evil" in itself, so he thinks he has to restore the "world" without the "evil." Levine kills himself, but the "world" still is; the quartermaster general sheds tears over the "world" that he believes he can bear, but he does not know what it is; the runner cannot but laugh in the "world" where his will to "do something" vainly survives. What is common to all three, or what is represented by the "trinity of conscience," is vanity. Levine, the pilot with high ideals, dies in the latrine; the quartermaster general's tears and the runner's laughter are set in a parodic image of homoerotic piéta and ironized by the situation that neither of them understands. Throughout the novel, no single conscience stands up in glory.

However, this vanity is the very essence of what Faulkner calls in his prefatory note to *A Fable* the "fire" to fight fire. It is ridiculous to interpret this "fire" as nuclear missiles launched against the perpetrators of nuclear war. Faulkner is radically ironical; he sounds more like referring to the fire of God's wrath, which is frequently mentioned in the Bible.[13] By the "fire" to fight fire, then, Faulkner means God's fire. Of course any human fire cannot pretend to be God's fire. It is vain to do so. Rather, the "fire" is this sense of vanity directed toward the vanity of warmongers who pretend to be God. Faulkner's irony is the same irony as we see in Ecclesiastes which begins with "vanity of vanities; all is vanity" (1: 2), a book which I suspect to be a hidden source which inspired Faulkner with the pessimistic overtone in *A Fable*. What "must be taught," Faulkner seems to suggest, is what is taught by Solomon:

> All *things* have I seen in the days of my vanity: there is a just *man* that perisheth in his righteousness, and there is a wicked *man* that prolongeth *his life* in his wickedness. Be not righteous over much, neither make thyself over wise: why shouldest thou destroy thyself? Be not over much wicked, neither be thou foolish: why shouldest thou die before thy time? (Ecclesiastes 7: 15–17)

Is the runner or the quartermaster general a "wicked *man* that prolongeth *his life* in his wickedness"? Is Levine "righteous over much" or "over wise," that is, the one who destroys himself? Or is he "over much wicked," or "foolish," that is, the one who dies before his time? Or is it the civilization itself that is a "wicked *man* that prolongeth *his life* in his wickedness"? Or is it war in general? Or even peace? Any association sounds plausible, since from the beginning the word "vanity" makes everything look equal. This is how vanity works, and what Faulkner calls the "fire" to fight fire is meant to work that way.

In the novel, Sutterfield makes the above point. Telling the story of the horse theft, Sutterfield tells the runner that the runner's laughter will be treated as equal by God with someone else's tears:

> 'What else can I do but laugh?' the runner said. 'Hadn't
> He rather have that than the tears?'
> 'He's got room for both of them. They're all the same to
> Him; He can grieve for both of them.' (Faulkner, *A Fable*
> 170)

Like Nancy in *Requiem for a Nun*, Sutterfield tells the runner that he "can believe" (169). Unlike Temple who only asks Nancy what and how, however, the runner criticizes Sutterfield's belief for its being ineffective against war, comparing him to a doctor who keeps saying to his patient to believe. What he needs, the runner tells Sutterfield, is a "surgeon," one who can see "blood" (171). The runner's radical conscience is clarified here. Later, the runner finds in the corporal the model "surgeon." In a sense, the runner is right, because unlike the "doctor" who just says, "Believe and hope. Be of good cheer," the corporal actually leads the mutiny. However, unlike the runner's "surgeon," the corporal does it non-violently, with no blood. On the contrary, the runner leads his mutiny like the "surgeon," like "someone already used to blood." Before the mutiny, on his way to Sutterfield and later to the sentry, the runner hurts several guards with the flat of his pistol. After he knocks down the fifth, the runner says to both Sutterfield and the sentry, who are worrying if the guard is dead, that he has learned to knock people down without killing them. Although no one dares try to make sure, some of those who are knocked down by the runner seem dead. If we call the runner "righteous," Sutterfield is as "righteous" as the runner is. Although Sutterfield believes in God who "can grieve for both" laughter and tears, and behaves like a moderate pacifist who simply believes and hopes, he eventually follows the runner. Sutterfield speaks for

Solomon's wisdom of vanity, but betrays Solomon's, or even his own, wisdom with his own death. With his death, he only adds another example to the vain death of a "just *man* that perisheth in his righteousness."

However, in *A Fable*, the one who best represents the wisdom of vanity is the old general. By the "hermaphroditism" of war, he means its vanity. What looks like his cynicism or pessimism, therefore, is his Solomon-like wisdom. The old general's knowledge of "hermaphroditism" of war is based on his clairvoyant knowledge—though anachronistic—of the results of World War II, the results more devastating than those of the previous world war. As we have seen in the beginning of this chapter, the old general's imagination describing the end of the world, "last ding dong of doom had rung and died," echoes Faulkner's own words written for his Nobel Prize acceptance speech; the old general's knowledge reflects Faulkner's own knowledge after World War II. Here is a clue to understanding Jewishness in *A Fable*.

As Godden points out, although the "word 'Jew' is unused in *A Fable*" (48), the novel abounds in references to Jewishness.[14] Referring to Zygmunt Bauman's *Modernity and the Holocaust*, Godden argues that Jewishness in *A Fable* designates the "conceptual Jew" (44), or the "Other" in general, an "alien who defines the power elite, the military body, and the citizens of a militarized state— defines each of them (in serial relation to one another) as dedicated to expelling the alien, which alien makes them what they are" (54). Referring also to Rudolph Rummel's concept of "democide"— "'public murder by governments acting authoritatively' outside the immediate context of war" (69)—, Godden further defines the "conceptual Jew[s]" as the victims of "democide," and suggests the possibility that the victims of the second mutiny by the runner might be regarded, though not without conditions, as the victims of "democide. Godden even extends the list of the victims to the victims of Hiroshima. Then Jewishness in *A Fable* signifies the mark of every citizen who might possibly become a victim of "democide," and, as

Godden emphasizes, it must be hidden because it does not fit the ideology of the time, that is, the Cold War militarism, especially its nuclearism.[15] Likewise, hermaphroditism must be hidden in *A Fable*, because, as the old general cynically or pessimistically suggests, it signifies the vanity of war.

Ironically, Jewishness and hermaphroditism are warned respectively by the runner who causes a massacre which looks like—though not strictly—a "democide" or the old general who perpetrates war. The runner and the old general, in this sense, make an ally of radicals. They radicalize the irony which Faulkner meant by the "fire" to fight fire. Jewishness and hermaphroditism are warnings against war. But when turned over, or radicalized, they cause and propel war. On the other hand, the old general shares with the corporal an understanding of the human mortality, which, in spite of his job to serve the human immortality, he has kept deep in his heart since he left Paris for Africa after graduating from the Academy, or even since he entered the Academy at seventeen, when he first held the idea of Paris as his heritage to bequeath to an heir. Offered that "heritage" by the old general, the corporal asks, "So we ally—confederate . . . . Are you that afraid of me?" (295) Perhaps the corporal does not understand what is truly offered by the old general. It is not the "heritage," or the power to sustain the human immortality, that is offered. It is rather the wisdom of the hermaphroditism of war, or of victory and defeat, or of mortality and immortality. Standing between the runner's extreme radicalism, which instigates war, and the corporal's radical pacifism, which stops war, the old general represents the hermaphroditism itself.

A Jonah's Objection: *Somersault*

In Oe's *Chugaeri*, or *Somersault*, we can certainly hear an echo of Faulkner's idea of "time [as] a fluid condition which has no existence except in the momentary avatars of individual people." Patron tells Kizu of the original idea which started the church:

案内人_{ガイド}は、根本の教義を私に理解させてくれた。唯一
者から光が放射されてこの世界が生じた、その光の粒
子/波動を、私らが個々の身体・精神のうちに持ってい
る、そしてそれはやがて唯一者に向けて還る、という
ものです。

　私らは個の自分を主体だと考えているが、私らひと
りひとりは唯一者から流出した光の粒子/波動のための、
運搬用の容器にすぎない。(上 272)

I learned the basic doctrine from Guide. The world came
into being when a light was emitted from the Almighty. We
all have in our bodies and minds the particles/waves of the
light. Eventually, however, those particles/waves return to
the Almighty.

　We usually think that we are individuals, the subjects,
but the truth is that we are nothing but the containers
carrying those particles/waves of light emitted from the
Almighty.[16]

Strictly speaking, the church's starting idea is Guide's, not Patron's.
Patron only meditates, and in his meditation, or trance, he only sees
"a white glower" 白くボーッと光るもの (上 206). As prophet, Guide
gives words to what Patron sees in his meditation, or what he
experiences through meditation. Patron says that he is even
influenced by Guide's idea:

案内人_{ガイド}はそういった。じつはそれが私にはよくわかっ
ていたとはいえないのですが・・・そして光の粒子/波
動が唯一者に還る時、その一粒は私らの身体を脱ぎ棄
てる。のみならず、同じように精神からも離脱するが、
それで私らの個が使用ずみの容器として棄てられるの
ではない。私らの個の魂は、その光の粒子/波動そのも
のとなって唯一者に還って行く。そういうのです。よ

くわからないままに、私はこの考えが好きでした。(上 273)

Guide said so. But I can't say I really understood what he said. When those particles/waves of light return to the Almighty, each of them casts off its body. It also separates itself from each mind, but that does not mean that we are thrown away like used containers. Each of our spirits returns to the Almighty as individual particle/wave. That's what he said. I liked the idea, though I couldn't understand it well.

While the similarity between Guide's idea of the Almighty and Faulkner's idea of time is apparent, the difference between the two should not be dismissed. Faulkner says that the fluid time has no existence in itself, whereas Guide imagines the existence of the whole entity of time to which every individual spirit or soul belongs, and calls it the Almighty. Herein lie already, even from the very beginning, the seeds of later deviation of the church into radicalism, a radicalism which eagerly seeks the return to or the unification with the whole entity of time by hastening the end of time, or of the world.

In *A Fable*, the old general's idea of man's immortality is a misconception of Faulkner's idea of the fluid time. The old general is a hermaphrodite who feels an affinity for the fluid time, which is represented by the corporal's mortality or ephemerality, but, at the same time, serves man's immortality, which in itself harbors the hermaphroditism of war, the "principles of victory and of defeat." While serving man's immortality, the old general knows that he is practically leading the whole humankind to its end, since man's immortality means nothing but the repetition, or the vicious circle, in which men keep vainly killing each other forever. The old general is a hermaphrodite in the sense that he is split between the feminine mortality, which warns the humankind against such a vicious circle, and the masculine immortality, which leads the humankind to the vicious circle. Man's immortality practically means the end of time, or the end of the world.

Similarly, in *Somersault*, Patron and Guide are two hermaphrodites, in the sense that their—strictly speaking, Guide's—original idea for their church includes both the like of the idea of "fluid time" and the like of the idea of man's immortality. Like the old general, Patron and Guide sense the "fluid time," but, at the same time, work for the end of world. However, there is a slight difference between Patron's and Guide's views of time. Originally, Patron had an idea closer to that of the fluid time, though he can express it only after he is influenced by Guide's verbalism:

> じつのところ私には、個としての自分の世界の終りの
> 認識、個としての自分の悔い改めのみでよかった。個
> として神と繋がる時を持つだけで、私は不満も恐怖も
> 抱かず死んでゆけるはずでした。死の後の、魂の救い
> ということも考えないほどだった。いまからさらに、
> ある期間は生き延びることになる。その間、近づきつ
> つある世界の終りを、個として明らかに認識して、個
> として悔い改める。そしてできうれば、神秘主義者の
> 隠者のように神との個の関係のうちにあって死ぬ。(上
> 285–86)

> To tell the truth, all I wanted was the sense of the end of the world, the end of me as an individual, or repentance as an individual. I expected to die after spending a little time in a personal relationship with God, without any discontents or fears. I wasn't even expecting my soul to be saved after death. I am going to live for a while. In the meantime, I want to repent as an individual, feeling the end of the world approaching, especially to me as an individual. And if possible, I want to die like a mystical hermit, in a personal relationship with God.

Here we can even hear an echo of Eula's "You just are" in *The Town*, and also Temple's skepticism in *Requiem for a Nun* concerning what or how to believe. On the other hand, though he basically agrees with Patron, Guide wants more than to be merely personal, to be more active in leading others to the end of the world, which is common to every human being:

> 救い主の神との繋がりは、個としてのもの。私たちが
> 悔い改めることによって神との間に開く関係も、個と
> してのもの。しかし私たちが教団の活動を重ねること
> で、大きい瞑想のヴィジョンに示された世界の終りを
> 社会へと押し出し、悔い改めを徹底して呼びかけるな
> らば、私たちの個としての神との関係を超えたものが
> そこに現われるだろう。それが救い主の根本の教えで
> す。預言者としての私は、その活動をやってゆく自分
> らの、悔い改めた人間としての質を高めることを希っ
> て、この研究所を設立したのです。(上 298)

The Savior's connection with God is personal. So is the relationship with God that we begin by repenting. However, if we do more things as a church, try harder to show our meditated vision of the end of the world to the society, and seriously call for its repentance, something beyond a personal relationship with God will appear. That is the basic doctrine of the Savior. As Prophet, I myself wanted to better the quality of each personality, as a person who has repented through our activities. That is why I founded this research institute.

To provide a place for the young people who joined their church with "spiritual crisis" 魂の不安 (上 290), Guide starts the Izu Research Institute and, later, leads the radical faction of the church. Guide understands Patron's sense of being personal, being individual, but, at the same time, feels it his imminent task to vent the "spiritual unease" of those young people, and together serve the repentance of the whole humankind.

However, Patron and Guide together make a somersault, and repudiate the church itself when they realize that their radical faction has become extremely radical and planned terrorism on nuclear power plants. This is the equivalent of the old general's leaving Paris, and also of the corporal's mutiny. The old general and the corporal together make a somersault in the midst of the western history, and say no to the realization of man's immortality, which is nothing but the end of the world. Ten years after the somersault, Guide is lynched by part of the former radical faction of the church. In *A Fable*, the corporal is executed by the old general, whose job is to hasten the end of the world by serving man and his folly. The corporal does not inherit from his father the "heritage," the service or even servitude to man's immortality. In *Somersault*, Ikuo inherits from Guide or even the radical faction of the church their radical apocalypticism, though at the end of the novel he pretends to agree with Patron. On the other hand, Kizu, the focal character, succeeds to Guide as Patron's prophet, though he succeeds more to Patron's idea of being individual, and opposes Ikuo. Both Ikuo and Kizu are practically homosexuals, and also metaphorically hermaphrodites in terms of their relationships to Patron and Guide.

As hermaphroditism in *A Fable* is concerned with the wisdom of that vanity expressed by war, hermaphroditism in *Somersault* leads both Kizu and Ikuo to a wisdom concerning the vanity of human efforts to find the truth, or what God really wants. What war is in *A Fable* is in *Somersault* a religious questioning about the end of the world. Therefore, in *Somersault*, the choices are not victory or defeat, or war or peace, but whether to want the end of the world that God has ordained or not to want it. To want too eagerly the end of the world, or the idea of hastening the end of the world on the human part, leads one to radicalism. In *Somersault*, Ikuo is such a radical. Ikuo finds wisdom about vanity not in Ecclesiastes but in the book of Jonah, and radicalizes it. For Kizu, however, whether to want the end of the world or not has only a secondary importance; what is more important for him, as he tells Dr. Koga, is "to spend the rest of life with him" 人生の残りをあの若者と一緒に居たい (下 196). Kizu joins Patron's church in order to stay close to Ikuo. On Kizu's mind, his own imminent death by cancer weighs more than the end of the world. However, Kizu is even ambiguous, or metaphorically hermaphroditic, concerning whether he wants to be cured or not; he is neither "entirely denying" "Patron's spiritual power to effect a cure," nor "clinging to it as his last hope" 師匠（パトロン）の魂の力の治療ということを・・・まったく受けつけないのではありません。しかし、それに期待してすがりつく、ということもありません (下 196). Kizu calls his life "my ambiguous life as painter" 中途半端な画家の人生 (下 196).

As we have seen in the previous chapter, Oe worked on the revision of his narrative technique, or a "gender trouble," through the 1980s, especially in the two novels published in 1989 and 1990, that is, *An Echo of Heaven* and *A Quiet Life* respectively. In the former, Oe lets his female protagonist criticize the authenticity of Oe's recurrent first person male narrator, and in the latter, a female narrator—the daughter of the novelist K, Oe's persona—deconstructs her father's language and reveals its dependence on the feminine. Oe's novels of the 1990s follow those attempts: both the androgynous narrator of the Flaming Green Tree trilogy and the focal character's homosexuality in *Somersault* are the fruits of Oe's "gender trouble" in the 1980s. Satchan, who narrates through the trilogy, is born as female, but lives as male until s/he converts to female at the beginning of his/her adolescence; in *Somersault*, Kizu realizes his homosexuality after his middle fifties. What is common to both Satchan and Kizu, as well as to Oe himself as a writer, is the realization that they are not genuinely male, or that their true gender or sexual identities have been hidden under their masculine guises that are socially given.

In *Somersault*, as a painter, Kizu is given the role of the eye in the novel. In this sense, Kizu exactly succeeds to Satchan, the narrator in the Flaming Green Tree trilogy. Indeed, Kizu is not the narrator; in his second attempt to narrate the story of a religious movement, Oe

switches from the first-person narration to the third-person. However, Kizu's role is identical with Satchan's in presenting a perspective split between the leader of the church and its radical faction.
Their difference lies in Kizu's death. At each end of the trilogy or
Somersault, the leader of the church—Brother Gii in the former and
Patron in the latter—dies a martyr. In *Somersault*, Kizu also dies.
Kizu cannot narrate the story, because he has to die in the end. At the
end of his life, Kizu wants to see Ikuo's erect penis for the last time,
and asks him for it. Ikuo shows it to him, but Kizu, who is losing his
sight, says, "Actually, I can't see well" 実ハ、良ク見エナインダ (下
558). Satchan in the trilogy narrates the story after everything, by
looking back at everything which has happened; for Kizu, on the
contrary, there is no looking back. The novel begins with Kizu's
meeting Ikuo, and ends with his leaving Ikuo; Kizu's confrontation
with Ikuo comprises the central plot of the novel.

    In *Somersault*, the motif of radicalism, represented by Ikuo, is as
important as that in *A Fable*. We cannot help wondering why Oe, after
the Flaming Green Tree trilogy, which he thought would be his last
novels, had to write *Somersault*, a novel with a plot similar to that
which he had treated in the trilogy, but with more an emphasis on the
motif of radicalism. On March 20, 1995, the radical faction of Aum
Shinrikyo, a Japanese cult, caused a terrorism on subway trains in
Tokyo, and killed eleven people by sarin, a nerve gas. There is no
doubt that this incident shook Oe's imagination, or soul. In
Somersault, Aum is frequently mentioned, and compared with
Patron's church. Just like the radical faction of Patron's church that
planned the attack on nuclear power plants, many of the members of
the radical faction of Aum who perpetrated the terrorism were
scientists or the graduates of prestigious universities with various
degrees and majors. Especially, among them was included Hayashi
Ikuo, medical doctor, who joined Aum with his wife and two children
in 1990 at the age of forty-two, resigned from a position in a hospital.
He was a graduate of the Keio University medical school, one of the
most prestigious medical schools in Japan. Perhaps he is the model of

Dr. Koga in *Somersault*, and the name Ikuo also originates with him. Among the arrested Aum members, Hayashi is best known for his repentance, self-denial, and the sense of guilt which he expressed during the ensuing trials.

What characterizes the members of Aum's radical faction—the center of which is believed to be Aum's leader or guru, Asahara Shoko (born Matsumoto Chizuo)—is their strong inclination toward the idea of the end of the world, especially the idea that the world-ending World War III is inevitable and imminent. To support the idea, Asahara liked to refer to the Christian idea of Armageddon, and also, to justify its radicalization, he referred to the Buddhist idea of Poa, which means, in his interpretation, to kill others to save their lives or "provide them with a favorable rebirth" (Lifton 8).[17] In *Somersault*, too, at the center of Patron's teachings is the idea that the end of the world is imminent. And like Aum, the radical faction of Patron's church plans to enlighten people on the idea of the end of the world by terrorism—by exploding nuclear power plants—, though the plan aborts because of Patron and Guide's somersault, their renunciation of the church as well as the idea of the imminent end of the world. After joining Patron's church, Ikuo soon approaches the former radical faction led by Dr. Koga. Both Kizu and Dr. Koga suspect that Ikuo was interested in a particular group of those remnants of the former radical faction, which Kizu calls "the true radicals of the former radicals" もと急進派のなかでもラディカルな連中 (下 107). Those are the ones who, even after ten years, still hold on to their radicalism, and torture Guide to death.

The very first episode of the novel, in which the ten-year-old Ikuo destroys a model city made by plastic pieces at an exhibition of the imaginary landscape of the future, foreshadows his later radical personality, which Dr. Koga calls a "Jonah-type personality" ヨナ的な人格 (下 109). However, Ikuo has been aware of it himself. Ikuo destroys the city already thinking of Jonah. When Ikuo meets Kizu at the athletic club fifteen years after the incident, he confesses, "ever since I was a child, the book of Jonah has bothered me" 子供の時分か

ら「ヨナ書」のことが、気にかかっているものですから (上 74). What
bothers Ikuo most in the book of Jonah is God's turnover, or
somersault. Ikuo believes that God should make another, reverse
somersault, and destroy Nineveh. Hence Ikuo's questioning "if the
book of Jonah really ends like that" あれで「ヨナ書」が本当に終って
るのかどうか (上 74). Later, for the theme of the third panel of the
triptych which Kizu is creating based on the book of Jonah, Ikuo
proposes a scene which should replace the present ending of the book,
a scene in which "God stands side by side with Jonah, looking down
at the burning city of Nineveh, the destruction of which He has once
given up but now has resumed"; いったんは断念したニネベの全面破
壊をやりとげることにして、燃え上がる都市をヨナと並んで見おろし
ている(下 206). Patron tells Kizu of the question Ikuo asked him in
their first meeting: "Ikuo's question to me was simple: Was God right
in canceling His order for Jonah to work for Him, to work for His
decision to destroy a city? Ikuo looked like speaking for Jonah"; 育男
君の私への問いかけは単純で、いったん神がひとつの都市を滅ぼすと
決意して、そのために働けと命じておいてから、それを取り消すのは
正しいのか、というものでした。ヨナの代訴をするふうでしたよ(下
390). For Ikuo, as he asks Kizu to "have Patron in the painting as God,
who has just been persuaded by Jonah's protest" 師匠〔パトロン〕に、ヨナの抗議
に説得された主として、画面に入って来てもらいたかった(下 206),
Patron is God, or, at least, one who is expected to mediate between
Ikuo and God. Ikuo's question to Patron, therefore, is his Jonah-like
challenge to God.

What bothers Ikuo in the book of Jonah is the sense of vanity, the
vanity to follow God, or even live in the world where God is inconsistent. However, Ikuo makes his own somersault here. He turns
the sense of vanity into a chance for human freedom.[18] Ikuo says:

その上で、あきらめて神の命じることをやる気になる。
いったんそう決心すると、頑固になる。方針を変えた
神に異議を申し立てて、初めに定めたことをやりぬく
べきじゃないか、と詰る。これこそ自由な人間らしい

やり方じゃないですか？神がある、ということに支え
られている自由でもあるけれど。そしてこれは私の間
違いかも知れませんが、神の方でも、そのように異議
を申し立てるやつのいう自由を考えにいれるのでなく
ては、広大無辺な本当の自由は確かめられないのじゃ
ないか？(上 83)

He finally gives up and decides to do as God orders him.
Once he makes up his mind, however, he becomes stubborn.
He makes an objection to God, and tells God that He should
do as He first planned. This is exactly the way a free person
should act, isn't it? I know that, in a sense, humans are free
because they were made by God to be free. However,
though I might be wrong, can God Himself be sure if His
freedom is really unlimited? To make sure of that, doesn't
He have to take into consideration the freedom of human
objection?

Ikuo considers Jonah's objection to God, or his demand for God's
consistency, as a sign of human freedom. Ikuo sounds almost like
Patron in suggesting a personal relationship to God. However, Ikuo is
more like Guide in emphasizing God's control over each personal
freedom, or God's knowledge of what "unlimited freedom" is. Ikuo's
idea of freedom, then, is another expression of Guide's desire to
clarify the presence of God through the realization of the end of the
world. Here Ikuo suggests two different Jonahs: the Patron-like Jonah
and the Guide-like Jonah. For the Patron-like Jonah, his being able to
freely and personally object to God is more important than knowing
what God is or what God really wants. On the contrary, for the
Guide-like Jonah, God's being certainly there and giving orders to the
repentant in a reasonable way is more important than his being free.

Ikuo's questioning makes us realize that the old general and the
corporal in *A Fable* are also those two different Jonahs. The old
general is the Guide-like Jonah, who, like Guide who speaks for

Patron, speaks for the corporal, and, at the same time, like the Jonah who demands that God's first plan to destroy Nineveh should be completed, sticks to the idea of man's immortality, which leads to the end of the world. On the other hand, the corporal is the Patron-like Jonah, who, like the Jonah who disobeyed God's order to tell the Ninevites of their destruction, quietly stands up against war or the course leading to the end of the world, and, also like Patron who at the end of the novel dies a martyr to warn against the re-radicalization of the church, dies a martyr to warn against the illusion of man's immortality which means nothing but an overall destruction of humankind. However, we should note here that, like the Jonah who escaped from God's order to tell the Ninevites of their destruction, the old general once escaped from Paris, and stayed in Africa and Tibet, which are the equivalents for the big fish's belly, where Jonah stayed for three days and three nights. Then, also like the Jonah who went to Nineveh and told the city their doom, the old general returns to Paris, and serves a war.

At the end of *Somersault*, Kizu dies after telling Ikuo that "even without God, I would say *rejoice*" オレハ、神ナシデモ、rejoice トイ ウヨ (下 558). Repeating what Kizu said to him, Ikuo sheds tears. Here, just as in the ending of *A Fable*, laughter and tears commingle, though in *Somersault*, the one who laughs is the one who bears the world, and the one who cries is the one who holds on to his radicalism. In *A Fable*, Sutterfield foretells that the runner's laughter will be treated equally by God with someone else's tears; in fact, the laughter of the runner, who follows the corporal, though in a radical way, is commingled with the tears of the quartermaster general, who understands the old general most. In *Somersault*, Ikuo, Guide's heir, responds to the atheistic laughter of Kizu, Patron's heir, with his tears. In addition to Ikuo and Kizu's commingling, the faction called the Quiet Women give up their wish to go to heaven, and "have been in a good relationship with the local women" 地域の女性たちと良い関係 にある (下 551). Like Levine, the pilot who died in the latrine, the Quiet Women who wished to ascend to heaven end up in the "Valley

Where Twenty-Five Elegant Ladies Shat" 二十五人もの上品なオナゴ
シがクソした沢. At the end of the novel, apart from whether God
exists or not, a "trinity of conscience"—the Quiet Women, Kizu, and
Ikuo—dissolves into a vanity similar to that revealed at the end of *A
Fable.*

Ikuo inherits from Guide a penchant for the end of the world. Like
Guide, Ikuo believes that God, or what Guide calls the Almighty,
should prove His presence or His consistent will by bringing the
world to its end. On the other hand, through the homosexual relationship, or commingling, with Kizu, Ikuo also learns the vanity of
demanding God's consistency. Like the Jonah at the end of the present
book of Jonah, Ikuo at the end of the novel seems to be persuaded that
it is vanity to demand God's consistency, or try to haste the end of the
world on the human part. As we have seen, however, for Ikuo, vanity
is a chance for human freedom. For Ikuo, his homosexual relationship
with Kizu is such a chance. Ikuo falls into his second homosexual
relationship—that is, the relationship with Kizu—half willingly and
half hesitantly. Before he meets Kizu, Ikuo has already sensed a
vanity in a homosexual relationship, and since then, he has linked
his questioning about God's inconsistency to his ambiguous homosexuality. Since it makes him ask whether God exists or not, or what
God really wants, or what God wants to make him do, a homosexual
relationship is a chance to build a personal, or free, relationship with
God. However, it is not a personal religious feeling which Patron has;
rather, it is more like Guide's desperate search for the sense of
unification with the Almighty, or certainty of its presence. For Ikuo, a
homosexual relationship is a potential path to the realization of the
presence of God.

Ikuo's relationship with Mr. Schmidt starts when he is ten and a
half years old. It is soon after the relationship started that Kizu
happens to see Ikuo destroy the model city at the plastic model
competition. Later, at the age of fourteen, Ikuo hits Mr. Schmidt in the
back and thighs with a poker and makes him a man in a wheelchair
for the rest of his life. Two years later, Ikuo finally kills Mr. Schmidt.

Ikuo says that when he hit Mr. Schmidt at the age of fourteen he heard a "voice, not of his own, say, *Do it!*" 自分のものでない声が、ヤレ！と (下 261), and when he killed Mr. Schmidt at sixteen, he "remembered" 思い出していた (下 261) the voice of two years before. Ikuo also says that when he heard the voice at the age of fourteen, he "lacked the courage to carry out to the end" 自分には勇気がなくて、しまいまでやりとおせなかった and "tried to escape" 逃げようとした (下 261). For Ikuo, it was the voice of God, and he was well aware that he was like Jonah, who once escaped from God's voice, but later persistently stuck to the voice he had heard before. Then, at twenty-five, Ikuo meets Kizu and has a homosexual relationship for the first time after the relationship with Mr. Schmidt. Through the homosexual relationship with Kizu, Ikuo realizes for the first time that he had heard the voice when he destroyed the model city, though he admits that since he heard the voice at the age of fourteen, he has never heard it. Ikuo joins Patron's church expecting to hear the voice again through Patron.

The voice of God comes to Ikuo when he is in a homosexual relationship. It is the voice of Ikuo's hidden homosexual self. It tells Ikuo to kill Mr. Schmidt because Mr. Schmidt forced him into a homosexual relationship, and in so doing caused in him a repugnance against it. Ikuo might be too young to accept his homosexual self. At the age of fourteen, he escapes from the voice, but at the age of sixteen, he willingly tries to follow the order he heard two years before, even in face of the fact that God is silent this time. As Jonah protests against God who refrains from his previous plan, Ikuo protests against the silent God and kills Mr. Schmidt. Later, when he realizes Kizu's homosexual interest in him, Ikuo recalls the voice which has led him to kill Mr. Schmidt, but, at the same time, finds himself attracted to Kizu. However, even after having gotten used to the sexual relationship with Kizu, Ikuo still doubts whether he should keep going with the present relationship with Kizu, or why God is silent; Ikuo is probably afraid that Kizu might be another Mr. Schmidt who makes homosexuality repugnant. Similarly, Ikuo is attracted to

Patron because—even if he is not sexually attracted to Patron— Patron may make him hear the voice again, the voice which orders him to realize his homosexuality. However, when he realizes that Patron can no longer communicate with God, and, even worse, when Patron condemns him as "Faggot Satan!"男色家の悪魔！(下 469), Ikuo decides to leave the church—though he stays for a while to help Patron in the Spirit Festival.

After Patron's death, Ikuo marries Dancer and stays with the Church of the New Man. Ikuo is the new man; at least, he pretends to be so. At the end of the novel, Ikuo shows Kizu his erect penis, helped by Dancer, his wife. Kizu congratulates their marriage, and Ikuo thanks him. Ikuo no longer seems exclusively homosexual. At the same time, freed from his obsession with homosexuality, Ikuo no longer seems to need to hear the voice of God. After Kizu's death, as if to express his relinquishment of the idea of the end of the world, which has been the raison d'être for the radical faction of the church, Ikuo says that the church is the place where the matters of the soul are done. Before his death, Kizu has said: "Ikuo, do you still want to hear God's voice? You don't need God's voice, do you? We, humans, should be free"; 育雄、ヤハリ、神ノ声ガ聞コエナクテハ、イケナイカネ？神ノ声ハ、イラナイノジャナイカ？人間ハ、自由デアル方ガ、イイヨ(下 558).

Ikuo's words, in a sense, are an expression of homage to Kizu; Ikuo seems to have conceded to Kizu's atheism. However, what Kizu means by being free in his last words is different from what Ikuo has meant in their early conversation by Jonah's freedom, that is, "the freedom to object to what [God] wants." Has Ikuo changed his views? Speaking with Ikuo after Kizu's death, Ogi, whose role is to inherit Kizu's perspective, gets the impression that "Ikuo was not Jonah any more" 育雄はよなでなかった (下 550). But later, after seeing in Ikuo the "weird, uncontrollable Jonah unmasked" 手のつけられない奇怪さのよなが仮面を脱いだ, Ogi changes his views and thinks that Ikuo is a "man who is to be his mortal enemy" 自分には生涯の敵となる人間 (下 554). Perhaps Ikuo has not changed. Kizu's freedom is atheistic, whereas Ikuo's theistic. Similarly, Kizu's sexuality is atheistic, whereas Ikuo's theistic. Kizu insists that Ikuo should be free from his own suspicion about his true sexual self, or from his silent God, but, as Ikuo sees it in the book of Jonah, his freedom is possible only within the reach of God. Ikuo still wants to hear God's *"Do it!"* that is, the voice of his inner—repressed—homosexual self. God's *"Do it!"* has made the ten-year-old Ikuo destroy the model city and also made the sixteen-year-old Ikuo kill Mr. Schmidt. Ikuo's radical will to end the world runs parallel with, or is the projection of, his wish to punish everything which hinders his inner homosexual self. At the end of *A Fable*, vanity ironizes on both laughter and tears. Similarly, at the end of *Somersault*, vanity presides over both Kizu, the atheist, and Ikuo, a Jonah who objects to the inconsistent, silent God. However, just as the runner in *A Fable* keeps saying, "I'm not going to die," Ikuo keeps holding on to his radical apocalypticism. In *A Fable*, vanity of war, which is linked to hermaphroditism, is accompanied by the warning against "democide," which is expressed in the novel as hidden Jewishness. The runner's second mutiny is a radicalization of such a warning against "democide." Curiously enough, even in *Somersault*, such an accompanying element of Jewishness is not lacking.[19]

Guide is a victim of the atomic bombing on Nagasaki. He is radiated as a child, and also loses his mother there. Though he was born in a Catholic family, he leaves the church because he "read in the paper that a famous Catholic man of letters had an audience with Emperor Hirohito" この国のカトリックの有名な文化人が天皇に拝謁したと新聞で読んだ(上 347). In our understanding of "democide," and perhaps as well as in Oe's understanding of Hiroshima and Nagasaki, Hirohito is certainly one of those perpetrators of "'public murder by governments acting authoritatively' outside the immediate context of war." Guide comes to dream of the Second Coming of Jesus in Japan to show his greatness over Hirohito, but "since it didn't look like he could expect to see the Second Coming, he came up with the radical idea that they should create a substitute with their own

hands"; この分ではイエス・キリストは再臨しそうにないから、自分ら
の手でそれに替わる者を作り出そうじゃないかと、過激なことをもく
ろむようになった(上 347–48). If we want to identify an origin of
radicalism in Patron's church, this dream of Guide is certainly it.
Guide's reference is not only to Hiroshima and Nagasaki. He also
refers to the Holocaust. He is influenced by the discussion of a Jewish
scholar concerning the "Star of David, the symbol of the state of
Israel" 国家イスラエルの象徴としての「ダビデの星」(上 348). In the
discussion, the Star of David reminds the Jews of their "suffering and
death" 苦しみと死, that is, the "Jewish people's road to the gas
chamber" ユダヤ人の、ガス室に到る道; the star serves as the "symbol
of the state of Israel," the symbol of the "road to life and rebuilding"
生命と再建の道 (上 348–49). Through the activities of the church,
Guide expects to find a symbol which, like the Stars of David, all the
Japanese of his generation, who suffered from the recent mass
atrocities, can hold up "as lighting the way to life and regeneration."
It should not be the Emperor, however, though the Emperor is defined
in the Japanese postwar constitution as the symbol of the Japanese.
For Guide, the Emperor is the very one who is responsible for those
atrocities. Guide is also influenced by his father, a repatriate from
China, who told him through the mouth of his uncle who raised him
about the atrocities committed by Japanese troops in China. Guide
later tells Patron how his father thought when he knew of his wife's
death by the atomic bomb:

> どんな残虐行為も行なわなかった自分の、信仰厚い妻
> も、娘のような身空で赤んぼうを残して殺されていた。
> 自分は、これこそが神のおはからい、神の御業だと思
> う。ある場所で罪が行なわれる。罪に参加しなかった
> 者も、その場所にいたということのみで、同じく罪の
> ある者ではないか？さらにいえば、神が人間に大きい
> 罰をあたえる時、それは罪ある人間、罪のない人間を
> 問わないのではないか？なにより人間であることこそ
> が罰せられるのであるから。(上 358)

He'd committed no atrocities himself. But his wife, who
was devoted to her faith, was killed quite young, leaving
their baby behind. Then he thought: "This is exactly God's
will, God's doing. A sin was committed at a certain place,
and even if you did not commit it yourself, you are an
accomplice just because you were there. When God
severely punishes people, He would not distinguish the
sinful from the sinless. God punishes us because we are
what we are."

We can see here the connection between Guide's original radicalism
and Ikuo's Jonah-like objection to God's silence. Guide inherits from
his father a view of God, which Ikuo inherits from Guide. They both
face the God who treats every human being equally, tries to make
every human being feel unable to fathom God's will, and destroys a
city on behalf of every human being. Guide's Nagasaki is Ikuo's
Nineveh. What is common to both Guide and Ikuo is the sense of
vanity. They also share, however, the radicalism which is the result of
the radicalization of such a sense of vanity. Guide no longer asks
whether Truman was right or wrong, nor whether Hirohito was
responsible or not, since God does not distinguish between the
perpetrators of "democide" and its victims. Every one should be
punished.

In *A Fable*, Jewishness, which is supposed to imply the vanity of
war and warn against "democide," is hidden in the text, and even
repressed at the end of the novel under two voices. One is the voice of
the runner which declares his immortality. The other is the orator's
voice honoring the old general who lies dead in the casket: "That's
right, great general! Lie always with your face to the east, that the
enemies of France shall always see it and beware!" (368) The orator
does not recognize the irony implied here. We the readers know,
however, that the dead old general's face is uncannily pointed toward
the east—that is, Tibet, or "another country"—where he stayed after
escaping from Paris and even Africa, and begot the corporal. The

corporal, his son, is now lying beside him as the Unknown Soldier. Since it is not affected by this irony, the orator's voice sounds triumphant. The vanity, which the old general has known, is repressed under it.

In *Somersault*, too, the sense of vanity, which originates in Guide's sympathy with all the victims of Hiroshima and Nagasaki, the Holocaust, and the Japanese invasion of China, is overturned by Guide himself into radicalism, and finally hidden or repressed at the end of the novel under Ikuo's pretentious declaration that their church is dedicated to the "deeds of the soul." As Guide caused the deviation of the church into radicalism, Ikuo is now ready to do the same to the renewed Church of the New Man. At the ends of both *A Fable* and *Somersault*, vanity is repressed, and man's sense of immortality goes on.

As we have seen in Chapter One, Oe's Yoknapatawpha is an attempt to laugh at Japanese ultranationalism by degrading and lowering Japanese spiritual value symbolized by the Emperor. The "deeds of the soul," which Ikuo mentions at the end of *Somersault*, appear to be the antithesis to such a Japanese spirit, and therefore, serve Oe's purpose of criticizing it. In *Somersault*, however, Patron's personal religious feeling is distinguished from Guide's holistic search for the Almighty, and Ikuo is the heir to Guide. Even if it originated in a criticism against the Emperor, Guide's radicalism is identical with Japanese ultranationalism in the sense that they presuppose the precedence of the whole over each, to use Faulkner's phrases, "momentary avatar" of it. Patron's personal religion and Guide's radicalization correspond respectively to the corporal's mortality, or ephemerality, and the old general's immortality in *A Fable*. At the end of each novel, while those two parties commingle in the common sense of vanity, the voice of the radical, or man's immortality, represses such a sense of vanity. Under the disguise of his tears, Ikuo's "deeds of the soul" express his on-going radicalism, his wish to seek the end of the world. As the old general's spirit, or heart in conflict, ends up choosing man's immortality, Ikuo's soul, which is an amalgam of both Patron's and Guide's legacies, ends up suggesting its return to the idea of the end of the world. Set in the village modeled on Oe's native village in Shikoku, *Somersault*, so far, culminates Oe's own Yoknapatawpha novels. While we can say that Oe has succeeded in presenting a soul different from the ultranationalistic Japanese spirit, Oe does not seem to be laughing. On the contrary, as Faulkner lamented the lack of attention to the "problems of the spirit," Oe laments the lack of attention to the danger of deviation, or return to the Japanese spirit, which haunts the "matters of the soul."

Notes

1. To be more precise, according to Keen Butterworth, Faulkner puts aside *A Fable* in December 1947, and resumes working on it in the summer of 1952 (8–9). However, Butterworth points out that, when Faulkner put aside the novel in 1947, "a good deal of the book was in nearly final form" (8).

2. We should be aware, as Polk reminds us in his study on the dubious relationship between Faulkner's Nobel Prize speech and *A Fable*, that "fiction and non-fiction are different as to their intentions and purposes" ("Enduring *A Fable* and Prevailing" 118). Polk also asks, however, "how should he have addressed the younger aspirants to the Nobel Prize on the futility of it all when he, standing so successfully on the pinnacle in Stockholm, would himself have been the denial of his own nihilism?" (115) In our discussion, Faulkner's Nobel Prize speech will be treated as another text, as well as *A Fable*, in which Faulkner's nihilism, which we will call a sense of vanity, is expressed.

3. Kodat (2001) also points out the anachronism of *A Fable*, but in a different context. Kodat sees in *A Fable* a "collapse of the high modernist project" in the age of mass culture (93–94).

4. In a way, my view of *A Fable* is a revision of the views which are rejected by Butterworth: that is, the view that the novel's center is the corporal, and the view that the novel is a pacifist book. Butterworth writes: "if the reader

identifies the corporal too closely with the divine Christ, he is forced into a reading of the novel which Faulkner did not intend. By making this close identification, the reader is forced to conclude that the truth, the moral center of the novel, lies in the corporal, precisely because of his identification with the divine" (14); "What Schwartz and a number of other critics have failed to see is that *A Fable* is antiwar only insofar as it abhors the agonies and suffering caused by war. It does not condemn those who fight the war, nor those who direct it, in good faith for just cause. The novel recognizes that violence and conflict, no matter how regrettable, are unavoidable as long as man remains man" (15–16).

5. In the "trinity of conscience" which Faulkner mentioned in the interview with Jean Stein vanden Heuvel, the English battalion runner represents the radical third (Meriwether and Millgate 247). A similar, but not identical, expression can be seen in *Faulkner in the University* (Gwynn and Blotner 245–46).

6. Curiously enough, as youth, the old general is described as "girlish looking," "frail and fragile in the same way that adolescent girls appear incredibly delicate yet at the same time durable" (212). He is also likened to the "maiden who without hesitation or argument feed [sic] in advance with her maidenhood the ferryman who set her across the stream and into heaven" (213). Nancy Butterworth and Keen Butterworth comment: "Faulkner may be referring to one of the many legends that accumulated around the figure of Saint Ursula [sic], a Cornish princess who lived during the 3rd, 4th or 5th centuries A. D. In legend she was sent to France with an entourage of eleven thousand virgins. Their ship was blown off course and landed in Germany; subsequently they were slaughtered near Cologne by the Huns and Picts" (167–68).

7. In "Woman and the Feminine in *A Fable*" Polk points out the general male tendency in the novel—represented by Levine, Gragnon, the old general, the corporal, and the horse—to resist or escape from women, the feminine, sexuality and domesticity. But what is truly insightful in this essay is its suggestion of the ambiguity of male-female distinction in the novel: "As 'articulations' of 'two inimical conditions,' the father and son are one of the

novel's many hermaphroditic pairs. At the close of the novel they are laid together, the two 'inimical conditions' they represent no longer inimical but self-exhausted on their deathbeds, the body they now inhabit that of mother earth, the Arc de Triomphe's symbolic masculine bulk rising high above them. There are two piétas as the end of the novel—one, implied, is the martyred corporal safe and comforted at last at mother earth's breast; the other, more potent, that of the crippled and scarred battalion runner receiving the masculine comfort of the quartermaster general—masculine idealism, or fantasy, sucking yet again at the dry breast of the military" (202). On the other hand, Godden, while admitting his debt to Polk's essay, points out a hidden hermaphroditic, homoerotic and even scatological structure in *A Fable* and connects it with Jewishness that is also hidden in the novel. Godden calls the overall structure of the novel the "vaginal, anal, Judaic triangle" (70).

8. I followed Faulkner in his use of the term "man," for the very reason that in *A Fable* he seems, even if unintentionally, to let the term stand out and criticize its prejudiced connotation.

9. Fujihira asserts that "the corporal would rather be that *bird* than simply breathing, 'only here to hear it'" ("The Indestructible Voice" 137). Although Fujihira also points out that the corporal "is destined to be what embodies life itself and to be the subject incorporating hopes and human aspiration," she does not pay attention to the bird's, or the corporal's, mortality or ephemerality. Another discussion on the episode is found in Urgo's "Where Was that Bird? Thinking *America* through Faulkner," in which Urgo reads the episode as an illustration of Faulkner's "public warning against interpreting his texts as *representations* of their subject matter" (104). This seems relevant to my argument here that the episode is deconstructing its seeming representations of the old general and the corporal.

10. According to the quartermaster general, the old general goes to a Tibetan lamasery. That means that the old general was interested in the Tibetan Buddhism. He fails in the Buddhist discipline, however, and commits fornication. We do not know how he met the woman, nor what the woman, who according to Marthe had "something—whatever it was—in her that had

never been ours" (244), and her husband and two daughters, named Marthe and Marya, were doing in Tibet. The text does not tell much about this.

11. The old general foretells the corporal that they "can even exist side by side together in this one restricted arena, and could and would, had yours not interfered with mine" (Faulkner, *A Fable* 294). "This one restricted arena" means the "earth" which the old general claims to be his, whereas, according to the old general, the corporal's is an "esoteric realm of man's baseless hopes and infinite capacity—no: passion—for unfact." It is even ironical that now the corporal has interfered with the old general's earth by lying dead side by side with him.

12. The irony at the end of the novel in connection with the merging of laughter and cry is pointed out in Straumann (360–61).

13. For example: "Behold, it is come, and it is done, saith the Lord God; this is the day whereof I have spoken. And they that dwell in the cities of Israel shall go forth, and shall set on fire and burn the weapons, both the shields and the bucklers, the bows and the arrows, and the handstaves., and the spears, and they shall burn them with fire seven years: So that they shall take no wood out of the field, neither cut down any out of the forests; for they shall burn the weapons with fire: and they shall spoil those that spoiled them, and rob those that robbed them, saith the Lord God" (Ezekiel 39: 8–10).

14. Among the characters, Levine is a Jew. If Godden guesses right, the corporal is a "Polish Jew" (45). If the corporal is a Jew, either his father or mother, or both, are Jews. Godden argues quite convincingly that his mother is a Jew (45). That does not exclude the old general, an orphan whose origin is not certain, from his possible Jewishness. His dark vision of the future, which anachronistically refers to the knowledge of the atrocities of World War II, allows us to imagine, though anachronistically, that he might be one of the victims of those atrocities. Although he says to the corporal, "we are not two Greek or Armenian or Jewish" (Faulkner, *A Fable* 294), he sounds as if he is referring to the Jewish Holocaust during World War II (Godden 69). Godden also points out that Faulkner's use of the word "holocaust" in describing the crowd—"like victims being resurrected after a holocaust" (Faulkner, *A Fable* 110)—suggests his concern with the Holocaust (Godden

The "Problems of the Spirit"/ the "Matters of the Soul"   179

39). The Jewish Holocaust is called "genocide," as well as the Armenian genocide of 1915, which is often called the first genocide. It is tempting to suppose that Faulkner had in mind the concept of genocide when he marshaled the Greek, the Armenian, and the Jewish. For the definition of genocide, see Hinton 1–7. The word "genocide" was coined by Raphaël Lemkin, a Polish jurist, to describe the Holocaust. An authoritative—though often regarded as problematic—definition of "genocide" can be seen in Article II of the 1948 United Nations Genocide Convention.

15. Godden makes the point: "In 1954, that the Jew might conceptually be every U. S. citizen cannot be brought to articulation because the willingness of the government to kill him, or to persist in the production of the means to his destruction, is itself grounds for barely announceable grief" (77). Before Godden, Urgo has already made the point in explaining why Faulkner's prefatory note to *A Fable* was rejected by the publisher: "In 1954, war was known to bring death home and destruction abroad, but it was also associated with prosperity. . . . Faulkner's anti-authoritarian and insurrectionist stand on war would find no audience, not even with the man editing his novel about authoritarianism and insurrection. It was heresy, and it was suppressed" (*Faulkner's Apocrypha* 103).

16. All references to the original *Chugaeri* in this study are to Oe Kenzaburo, *Chugaeri* (Tokyo: Shinchosha, 2002). All translations are mine except for words like the "Almighty," "faggot," and the "Star of David," which I owe to Philip Gabriel's translation—Oe Kenzaburo, *Somersault* (New York: Grove Press, 2003).

17. Robert Jay Lifton's *Destroying the World to Save It: Aum Shinrikyō, Apocalyptic Violence, and the New Global Terrorism* provides us with a detailed analysis of Aum's radical apocalypticism. Lifton is known through his books on the psychology of both the perpetrators and the victims of the Holocaust and the nuclear attacks on Hiroshima and Nagasaki, such as *The Nazi Doctors* and *Death in Life: Survivors of Hiroshima*. Oe has admired Lifton's work for a long time, and personally known him since his first visit to America in 1965. Oe's report of meeting Lifton in 1990 is included in *Hiroshima no "seimei no ki."*

18. In the book of Jonah, Jonah expresses his sense of vanity and its obverse freedom twice by saying, "it is better for me to die than to live" (Jonah 4: 3, 8). The first time is when God "repented of the evil" (Jonah 3: 10) which He had planned to do on the city of Nineveh, and the second time when God made the gourd, which He had planted for Jonah, wither by a worm. David M. Gunn and Danna Nolan Fewell point out that "God *is* the worm" (142), and also present an argument, with which Ikuo would certainly agree: "What, for example, if the plant is a paradigm of Jonah himself? The plant's purpose was 'to save [*hassil*—deliver] Jonah from his discomfort [evil].' Jonah's purpose was to pronounce doom (evil) on evil Nineveh, but by doing so he delivered the city from the evil. The plant, however, proved ephemeral. Did the deliverance Jonah effected prove ephemeral too? That certainly seems to be what Jonah considered most likely, as he sat skeptically watching the city, waiting for its relapse" (144)."

19. Jewishness is even conspicuous in the novel. Oe reveals that he gained the idea of Patron's somersault from Gershom Scholem's book *Sabbatai Sevi: the Mystical Messiah 1626–1676* (*Sakoku shitewa naranai* 92–93). In *Somersault*, a Jewish reporter writes articles about Patron for *The New York Times*, comparing Patron with Sabbatai Zevi.

Conclusion

Oe's "I" and Faulkner's "*is*"

Even before his feminist turn of the 1980s, Oe had written his novels with emphasis on doubling, fictionality, metaphoricity, satire, grotesque realism, and the self-critical "I," which deconstructs the factuality or honesty of "I." For Oe, the creation of his own Yokna-patawpha is a project in which all those novelistic, that is, critical, tools are involved. Oe's own Yoknapatawpha, therefore, is not merely an expression of his regionalism or love of Faulkner, but, from the beginning, a means to criticize the Japanese authoritarian society, which the "I" of *shosetsu* is supposed to reflect, through the eyes of the novelist's self-critical "I."

Faulkner is the source of Oe's critical, or self-critical, imagination. Oe often criticizes the naiveté of those critics who identify his narrators or focal characters, especially fascistic young men who appear in Oe's earlier work, with Oe himself. This is the same naiveté with which some readers of Faulkner used to believe that Faulkner is a misogynist or a racist. Such a belief originates from identifying Faulkner with his male white characters, such as Bayard Sartoris, Quentin Compson, Thomas Sutpen, Ike McCaslin, Harry Wilbourne and Gavin Stevens. Those readers are blind not to the fact that those characters are fictional, but to the fact that Faulkner is also a fiction produced out of his own characters, or his own creation. To paraphrase Gavin, who says that "the son is father to the man," we can say that Gavin is father and Eula is mother to Faulkner. In other words, if we can say that the novel is an art of fictionality or mediation, we can also say that the novelist is a being who can emerge only by him/herself being fictionalized or mediated by his/her own creation. Oe's Faulkner is such a novelist, that is, a fiction *per se* in which he becomes both Gavin, the masculine, and Eula, the feminine.

As we have seen, not only *The Sound and the Fury* or *Absalom, Absalom!* but also *Requiem for a Nun, A Fable, The Town* and *The Mansion* can provide us with rich resources in understanding Oe's attempt to revise the persistent "I" of the Japanese *shosetsu*. Temple's feminine skepticism toward the male language, the distance between Gavin and Eula or Linda, and the old general's hermaphroditism have served as the models to understand Ma-chan's feminine "I" in *A Quiet Life*, "I"'s misrepresentation of Marie in *An Echo of Heaven*, and Ikuo's hermaphroditism in *Somersault*, respectively. In addition, but no less importantly, we have seen, here and there, Faulkner's "*is*" appear as the common ground on which criticism is leveled against "*was*," distancing, or the idea of immortality. Faulkner says that "*is*" means time in a "fluid condition which has no existence except in the momentary avatars of individual people." Here, Faulkner has had his own say on Western individualism. Faulkner's individualism is a criticism against a fixed or ordered time in which an individual exists only as "*was*." In her article "Faulkner and 'Faulkner,'" Kodat asks: "if Faulkner believed only in individual reality, then how can the late novels be read as conscious and coherent interventions into the very public and communal institution that was Jim Crow?" (194) Indeed, Faulkner's individualism may give a pretext for his notorious go-slowism. At the same time, however, Faulkner's individualism, represented as "*is*," is always the basis for his criticism of the views which confine an individual to the image of "*was*," power being one and Jim Crow another.[1] While the Japanese "I" lacks individualism, Oe's criticism of the Japanese "I" is based on the individualism that Faulkner expressed in the Jean Stein interview. If the Japanese "I" simply reflects the society, or an order which has already been established and in which an individual exists only as "*was*," Oe's criticism of "I" is an attempt to disrupt the established order of the Japanese society and restore the "*is*" of individual people.

This is thus not so much a study of Faulkner's influence on Oe as a comparison between the two writers. For a reader who is familiar with Faulkner but not with Oe, the Faulkner in this study may seem too Japanese. Conversely, for a reader who is familiar with Oe but not with Faulkner, the Oe here may seem too Faulknerian. This is, however, precisely the aim of comparative studies of literature, that is, to make the familiar look unfamiliar. Here, I agree with Miyoshi, who in his *Off Center: Power and Culture Relations between Japan and the United States* writes: "Neutralization also operates by distancing the menacing source. A strange text is acknowledged to be strange, and this tautology thrusts the text out of the reader's proximity" (10). Rather than calling the strange strange, this study aimed at creating a strange—feminine, hermaphroditic, or individualistic—connection between two male writers whose connection has been regarded as rather obvious, not strange.

Note

1. Another recent discussion on Faulkner's individualism, especially in comparison with Thomas Jefferson's, can be found in Nicolaisen (2001).

Bibliography

Althusser, Louis. *Writings on Psychoanalysis.* Trans. Jeffrey Mehlman. Ed. Oliver Corpet and François Matheron. New York: Columbia UP, 1996.

Baker, Charles. *William Faulkner's Postcolonial South.* New York: Peter Lang, 2000.

Bergson, Henri. *Time and Free Will: An Essay on the Immediate Data of Consciousness.* Trans. F. L. Pogson. Mineola: Dover Publications, Inc., 2001.

Blake, William. *Complete Writings with Variant Readings.* Ed. Geoffrey Keynes. Oxford: Oxford UP, 1966.

Bleikasten, André. *The Most Splendid Failure: Faulkner's* The Sound and the Fury. Bloomington: Indiana UP, 1976.

Blotner, Joseph. *Faulkner: A Biography.* 2 vols. New York: Random, 1974.

Brooks, Cleanth. *William Faulkner: The Yoknapatawpha Country.* New Haven: Yale UP, 1963.

———. *William Faulkner: Toward Yoknapatawpha and Beyond.* New Haven: Yale UP, 1978.

Butler, Judith. *Gender Trouble: Feminism and the Subversion of Identity.* New York: Routledge, 1999.

Butterworth, Keen. *A Critical and Textual Study of Faulkner's* A Fable. Ann Arbor: UMI Research Press, 1983.

Butterworth, Nancy, and Keen Butterworth. *Annotations to William Faulkner's* A Fable. New York: Garland Publishing, Inc., 1989.

Clarke, Deborah. *Robbing the Mother: Women in Faulkner*. Jackson: UP of Mississippi, 1994.

Crabtree, Claire. "Plots of Punishment and Faulkner's Injured Women: Charlotte Rittenmeyer and Linda Snopes." *Michigan Academician* 24.2 (1992): 527–39.

Donaldson, Susan V. "Reading Faulkner Reading Cowley Reading Faulkner: Authority and Gender in the Compson Appendix." *The Faulkner Journal* 7.1–2 (1991–1992): 27–41.

Davis, Thadious M. "Reading Faulkner's Compson Appendix: Writing History from the Margins." *Faulkner and Ideology: Faulkner and Yoknapatawpha 1992*. Ed. Donald M. Kartiganer and Ann J. Abadie. Jackson: UP of Mississippi, 1995. 238–52.

Derrida, Jacques. *Spurs: Nietzsche's Styles/Éperons: Les Styles de Nietzsche*. Trans. Barbara Harlow. Chicago: U of Chicago P, 1978.

Dor, Joël. *Introduction to the Reading of Lacan: The Unconscious Structured Like a Language*. Ed. Judith Feher Gurewich. New York: Other Press, 1998.

Douglass, Paul. *Bergson, Eliot, and American Literature*. Lexington: UP of Kentucky, 1986.

Eliade, Mircea. *Images and Symbols: Studies in Religious Symbolism*. Princeton: Princeton UP, 1991.

Enomoto, Masaki (榎本正樹). *Oe Kenzaburo no hachijyu nendai* (『大江健三郎の八十年代』[Oe Kenzaburo in the 1980s]). Tokyo: Sairyusha, 1995.

Faulkner, William. *Absalom, Absalom!* 1936. New York: Vintage International, 1990.

———. "Appendix: 1699-1945 the Compsons." *The Portable Faulkner*. Ed. Malcolm Cowley. New York: Viking, 1954. 733–56.

———. *Essays, Speeches & Public Letters*. Ed. James B. Meriwether. New York: Random, 1965, 2004.

———. *A Fable*. 1954. New York: Vintage, 1978.

———. *Flags in the Dust*. New York: Vintage, 1974.

———. *The Hamlet*. 1940. New York: Vintage International, 1991.

———. *If I Forget Thee, Jerusalem [The Wild Palms]*. 1938. New York:

Vintage International, 1995.

———. *The Mansion.* 1959. New York: Vintage, 1965.

———. "A Note on *A Fable.*" *The Mississippi Quarterly: The Journal of Southern Culture* 26 (1973): 416–17.

———. *Requiem for a Nun.* 1951. New York: Vintage, 1975.

———. *The Sound and the Fury.* 1929. New York: Vintage International, 1990.

———. "To the Youth of Japan." *Essays, Speeches & Public Letters* 82–85.

———. *The Town.* 1957. New York: Vintage, 1961.

———. "Upon Receiving the Nobel Prize for Literature." *Essays, Speeches & Public Letters* 119–21.

Fowler, Doreen. *Faulkner: The Return of the Repressed.* Charlottesville: U of Virginia P, 1997.

———. "'In Another Country': Faulkner's *A Fable.*" *Studies in American Fiction* 15.1 (1987): 43–54.

———. "Revising *The Sound and the Fury: Absalom, Absalom!* and Faulkner's Postmodern Turn." *Faulkner and Postmodernism: Faulkner and Yoknapatawpha, 1999.* Ed. John N. Duvall and Ann J. Abadie. Jackson: UP of Mississippi, 2002. 95–108.

Fowler, Doreen, and Ann J. Abadie, eds. *Faulkner and Women: Faulkner and Yoknapatawpha, 1985.* Jackson: UP of Mississippi, 1986.

Freud, Sigmund. *Beyond the Pleasure Principle.* Trans. James Strachey. New York: Norton, 1961.

Fujihira, Ikuko. "The Image of Hell, the Myth of Family, and the Paradox of Narrative in William Faulkner, Toni Morrison, and Oe Kenzaburo." *The Faulkner Journal of Japan* 1 (1999). 20 Nov. 2002. <http://www.senshu-u.ac.jp/~thb0559/fujihiraRevd.htm>.

———. "The Indestructible Voice of the British Battalion Runner in *A Fable.*" Gresset and Ohashi 127–46.

Fulton, Keith Louise. "Linda Snopes Kohl: Faulkner's Radical Woman." *Modern Fiction Studies* 34.3 (1988): 425–36.

Gidley, Mick. "The Later Faulkner, Bergson, and God." *Mississippi Quarterly: The Journal of Southern Culture* 37.3 (1984): 377–83.

Godden, Richard. "*A Fable* . . . Whispering about the Wars." *The Faulkner*

Journal 17.2 (2002): 25–88.

Gordon, Sarah. *Flannery O'Connor: The Obedient Imagination*. Athens: U of Georgia P, 2000.

Gresset, Michel, and Ohashi Kenzaburo, eds. *Faulkner: After the Nobel Prize*. Kyoto: Yamaguchi, 1987.

Gunn, David M., and Danna Nolan Fewell. *Narrative in the Hebrew Bible*. Oxford: Oxford UP, 1993.

Gwin, Minrose. *The Feminine and Faulkner: Reading beyond Sexual Difference*. Knoxvill: U of Tennessee P, 1990.

Gwynn, Frederick L, and Joseph L. Blotner, eds. *Faulkner in the University: Class Conference at the University of Virginia 1957–1958*. Charlottesville: U of Virginia P, 1959.

Hinton, Alexander Laban. "Introduction: Genocide and Anthropology." *Genocide: An Anthropological Reader*. Oxford: Blackwell, 2002. 1–24.

Hoffman, Frederick J., and Olga W. Vickery, eds. *William Faulkner: Three Decades of Criticism*. New York: Harcourt, Brace & World, 1963.

Hönnighausen, Lothar. *Faulkner: Masks and Metaphors*. Jackson: UP of Mississippi, 1997.

Irigaray, Luce. *Marine Lover of Friedrich Nietzsche*. Trans. Gillian C. Gill. New York: Columbia UP, 1991.

———. *The Way of Love*. Trans. Heide Bostic and Stephen Pluháček. London; New York: Continuum, 2002.

Irwin, John T. *Doubling and Incest/Repetition and Revenge*. Baltimore: Johns Hopkins UP, 1975.

Kang, Hee. "A New Configuration of Faulkner's Feminine: Linda Snopes Kohl in *The Mansion*." *The Faulkner Journal* 8.1 (1992): 21–41.

Kartiganer, Donald M., and Ann J. Abadie, eds. *Faulkner and Gender: Faulkner and Yoknapatawpha, 1994*. Jackson: UP of Mississippi, 1996.

Jung, C. G., and C. Kerényi. *Essays on a Science of Mythology: The Myth of the Divine Child and the Mysteries of Eleusis*. Trans. R. F. C. Hull. Princeton: Princeton UP, 1978.

Kimura, Akio. "*Absalom, Absalom!* and *Man'en Gannen no Futtoboru*."

Soundings (the publication of Soundings eigo eibeibungaku kai) 17 (1991): 173–95.

Kobayashi, Hideo (小林秀雄). *Motoori Norinaga.* Vol. 1. (『本居宣長』上). Tokyo: Shinchosha, 1992.

Kodat, Catherine Gunther. "Faulkner and 'Faulkner.'" *American Literary History* 15.1 (2003): 188–99.

———. "Writing *A Fable* for America." Urgo and Abadie 82–97.

Kofman, Sarah. *Nietzsche and Metaphor.* Trans. Duncan Large. Stanford: Stanford UP, 1993.

Lifton, Robert Jay. *Destroying the World to Save It: Aum Shinrikyō, Apocalyptic Violence, and the New Global Terrorism.* New York: Henry Holt and Company, 1999.

McHaney, Thomas L., ed. *Faulkner Studies in Japan.* Athens: U of Georgia P, 1985.

Meriwether, James, and Michael Millgate, eds. *Lion in the Garden: Interviews with William Faulkner, 1926–1962.* New York: Random, 1968.

Minter, David. *William Faulkner: His Life and Work.* Baltimore: Johns Hopkins UP, 1980.

Miyoshi, Masao. *Off Center: Power and Culture Relations between Japan and the United States.* Cambridge: Harvard UP, 1991.

Moreland, Richard C. *Faulkner and Modernism: Rereading and Rewriting.* Madison: U of Wisconsin P, 1990.

Mortimer, Gail L. *Faulkner's Rhetoric of Loss: A Study in Perception and Meaning.* Austin: U of Texas P, 1983.

Napier, Susan J. *Escape from the Wasteland: Romanticism and Realism in the Fiction of Mishima Yukio & Oe Kenzaburo.* Cambridge: Council on East Asian Studies, Harvard University, 1995.

Nicolaisen, Peter. "William Faulkner's Dialogue with Thomas Jefferson." Urgo and Abadie 64–81.

O'Donnel, Patrick. "Faulkner's Future Tense: A Critique of the Instant and the Continuum." *Faulkner in the Twenty-First Century: Faulkner and Yoknapatawpha 2000.* Ed. Robert W. Hamblin and Ann J. Abadie. Jackson: UP of Mississippi, 2003. 107–18.

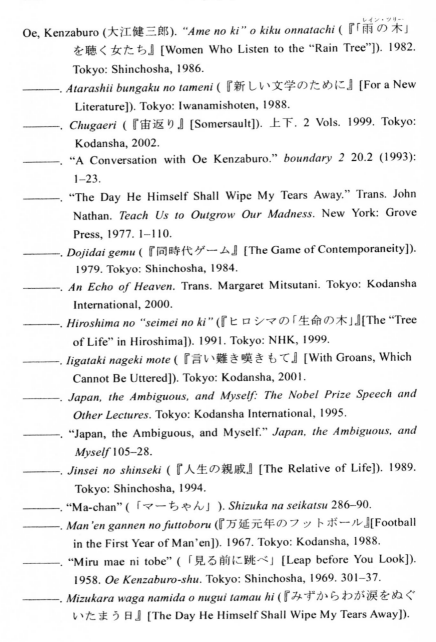

Oe, Kenzaburo (大江健三郎). *"Ame no ki" o kiku onnatachi* (『「雨 の 木」^{レイン・ツリー} を聴く女たち』 [Women Who Listen to the "Rain Tree"]). 1982. Tokyo: Shinchosha, 1986.

————. *Atarashii bungaku no tameni* (『新しい文学のために』 [For a New Literature]). Tokyo: Iwanamishoten, 1988.

————. *Chugaeri* (『宙返り』 [Somersault]). 上下. 2 Vols. 1999. Tokyo: Kodansha, 2002.

————. "A Conversation with Oe Kenzaburo." *boundary 2* 20.2 (1993): 1–23.

————. "The Day He Himself Shall Wipe My Tears Away." Trans. John Nathan. *Teach Us to Outgrow Our Madness.* New York: Grove Press, 1977. 1–110.

————. *Dojidai gemu* (『同時代ゲーム』 [The Game of Contemporaneity]). 1979. Tokyo: Shinchosha, 1984.

————. *An Echo of Heaven.* Trans. Margaret Mitsutani. Tokyo: Kodansha International, 2000.

————. *Hiroshima no "seimei no ki"* (『ヒロシマの「生命の木」』 [The "Tree of Life" in Hiroshima]). 1991. Tokyo: NHK, 1999.

————. *Iigataki nageki mote* (『言い難き嘆きもて』 [With Groans, Which Cannot Be Uttered]). Tokyo: Kodansha, 2001.

————. *Japan, the Ambiguous, and Myself: The Nobel Prize Speech and Other Lectures.* Tokyo: Kodansha International, 1995.

————. "Japan, the Ambiguous, and Myself." *Japan, the Ambiguous, and Myself* 105–28.

————. *Jinsei no shinseki* (『人生の親戚』 [The Relative of Life]). 1989. Tokyo: Shinchosha, 1994.

————. "Ma-chan" (「マーちゃん」). *Shizuka na seikatsu* 286–90.

————. *Man'en gannen no futtoboru* (『万延元年のフットボール』 [Football in the First Year of Man'en]). 1967. Tokyo: Kodansha, 1988.

————. "Miru mae ni tobe" (「見る前に跳べ」 [Leap before You Look]). 1958. *Oe Kenzaburo-shu.* Tokyo: Shinchosha, 1969. 301–37.

————. *Mizukara waga namida o nugui tamau hi* (『みずからわが涙をぬぐ いたまう日』 [The Day He Himself Shall Wipe My Tears Away]).

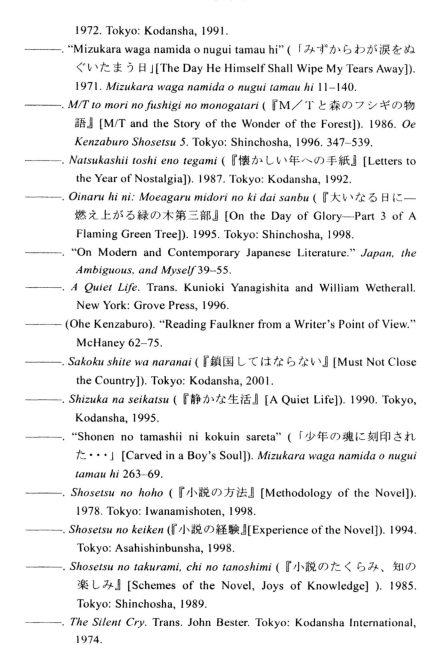

1972. Tokyo: Kodansha, 1991.

———. "Mizukara waga namida o nugui tamau hi" (「みずからわが涙をぬ ぐいたまう日」[The Day He Himself Shall Wipe My Tears Away]). 1971. *Mizukara waga namida o nugui tamau hi* 11–140.

———. *M/T to mori no fushigi no monogatari* (『M／Tと森のフシギの物 語』[M/T and the Story of the Wonder of the Forest]). 1986. *Oe Kenzaburo Shosetsu 5.* Tokyo: Shinchosha, 1996. 347–539.

———. *Natsukashii toshi eno tegami* (『懐かしい年への手紙』[Letters to the Year of Nostalgia]). 1987. Tokyo: Kodansha, 1992.

———. *Oinaru hi ni: Moeagaru midori no ki dai sanbu* (『大いなる日に— 燃え上がる緑の木第三部』[On the Day of Glory—Part 3 of A Flaming Green Tree]). 1995. Tokyo: Shinchosha, 1998.

———. "On Modern and Contemporary Japanese Literature." *Japan, the Ambiguous, and Myself* 39–55.

———. *A Quiet Life.* Trans. Kunioki Yanagishita and William Wetherall. New York: Grove Press, 1996.

——— (Ohe Kenzaburo). "Reading Faulkner from a Writer's Point of View." McHaney 62–75.

———. *Sakoku shite wa naranai* (『鎖国してはならない』[Must Not Close the Country]). Tokyo: Kodansha, 2001.

———. *Shizuka na seikatsu* (『静かな生活』[A Quiet Life]). 1990. Tokyo, Kodansha, 1995.

———. "Shonen no tamashii ni kokuin sareta" (「少年の魂に刻印され た・・・」[Carved in a Boy's Soul]). *Mizukara waga namida o nugui tamau hi* 263–69.

———. *Shosetsu no hoho* (『小説の方法』[Methodology of the Novel]). 1978. Tokyo: Iwanamishoten, 1998.

———. *Shosetsu no keiken* (『小説の経験』[Experience of the Novel]). 1994. Tokyo: Asahishinbunsha, 1998.

———. *Shosetsu no takurami, chi no tanoshimi* (『小説のたくらみ、知の 楽しみ』[Schemes of the Novel, Joys of Knowledge]). 1985. Tokyo: Shinchosha, 1989.

———. *The Silent Cry.* Trans. John Bester. Tokyo: Kodansha International, 1974.

————. *Somersault*. Trans. Philip Gabriel. New York: Grove Press, 2003.

————. *Warera no jidai* (『われらの時代』 [Our Age]). 1959. Tokyo: Shinchosha, 1963.

————. *Watashi to iu shosetsuka no tsukurikata*. 1998. (『私という小説家の作り方』 [How to Make a Novelist called "I"]). Tokyo: Shinchosha, 2001.

Oe, Kenzaburo, and Edward W. Said. "Sei no owari o mitsumeru sutairu" (「生の終りを見つめるスタイル」 [A Style with Which We Gaze at the End of Life]). *Sekai* Aug. (1995): 22–41.

Oe, Kenzaburo, and Subaru Henshuubu (大江健三郎、すばる編集部). *Oe Kenzaburo: saihakken* (『大江健三郎・再発見』 [Oe Kenzaburo: A Rediscovery]). Tokyo: Shueisha, 2001.

Ohashi, Kenzaburo. "'Native Soul' and the World Beyond: William Faulkner and Japanese Novelists." *Faulkner: International Perspectives: Faulkner and Yoknapatawpha, 1982*. Ed. Doreen Fowler and Ann J. Abadie. Jackson: UP of Mississippi, 1984. 257–75.

Polk, Noel. "Enduring *A Fable* and Prevailing." Gresset and Ohashi 110–26.

————. *Faulkner's Requiem for a Nun: A Critical Study*. Bloomington: Indiana UP, 1981.

————. "Woman and the Feminine in *A Fable*." Fowler and Abadie 180–204.

Rio-Jelliffe, R. *Obscurity's Myriad Components: The Theory and Practice of William Faulkner*. Lewisburg: Bucknell UP, 2001.

Roberts, Diane. "Eula, Linda, and the Death of Nature." *Faulkner and the Natural World: Faulkner and Yoknapatawpha, 1996*. Ed. Donald M. Kartiganer and Ann J. Abadie. Jackson: UP of Mississippi, 1999. 159–78.

————. *Faulkner and Southern Womanhood*. Athens: U of Georgia P, 1994.

Said, Edward W. "Yeats and Decolonization." *Culture and Imperialism*. 1993. New York: Vintage, 1994. 220–38.

Sartre, Jean-Paul. "Time in Faulkner: *The Sound and the Fury*." Trans. Martine Darmon. Hoffman and Vickery 225–32.

Schreiber, Evelyn Jaffe. "What's Love Got to Do With? Desire and Subjectivity in Faulkner's Snopes Trilogy." *The Faulkner Journal* 9.1–2 (1993–1994): 83–98.

Slaughter, Carolyn Norman. *"Absalom, Absalom!*: 'Fluid Cradle of Events (Time).'" *The Faulkner Journal* 6.2 (1991): 65–84.

Snyder, Stephen, and Philip Gabriel. Introduction. *Oe and Beyond: Fiction in Contemporary Japan*. Ed. Stephen Snyder and Philip Gabriel. Honolulu: U of Hawai'i P, 1999. 1–10.

Straumann, Heinrich. "An American Interpretation of Existence: Faulkner's *A Fable*." Hoffman and Vickery 349–72.

Tomioka, Taeko, and Oe Kenzaburo (富岡多恵子、大江健三郎). "Kotoba soshite bungaku e" (「言葉そして文学へ」[From Language to Literature]). *Gunzo* Aug. (1985): 136–62.

Towner, Theresa M. *Faulkner and the Color Line: The Later Novels*. Jackson: UP of Mississippi, 2000.

Trouard, Dawn. "Eula's Plot: An Irigararian Reading of Faulkner's Snopes Trilogy." *Mississippi Quarterly* 42.3 (1989): 281–97.

Tsushima, Yuko (津島佑子). "Jinsei to shosetsu" (「人生と小説」[The Life and the Novel]). *Shincho* 86.6 (1989): 286–89.

Tsushima, Yuko, and Oe Kenzaburo (津島佑子、大江健三郎). "Sozoryoku to joseitekina mono" (「想像力と女性的なもの」[Imagination and the Feminine]). *Sekai* Aug. (1985): 136–52.

Urgo, Joseph R. *Faulkner's Apocrypha: A Fable, Snopes, and the Spirit of Human Rebellion*. Jackson: UP of Mississippi, 1989.

———. "Where Was that Bird? Thinking *America* through Faulkner." Urgo and Abadie 98–115.

Urgo, Joseph R, and Ann J. Abadie, eds. *Faulkner in America: Faulkner and Yoknapatawpha, 1998*. Jackson: UP of Mississippi, 2001.

Watson, James Gray. *The Snopes Dilemma: Faulkner's Trilogy*. Coral Gables: U of Miami P, 1970.

Williams, David. *Faulkner's Women: The Myth and the Muse*. Montreal: McGill-Queen's UP, 1977.

Wilson, Michiko N. *The Marginal World of Oe Kenzaburo: A Study in Themes and Techniques*. Armonk, NY: Sharpe, 1986.

Wondra, Janet. "'Play' within a Play: Gaming with Language in *Requiem for a Nun*." *The Faulkner Journal* 8.1 (1992): 43–59.

Yamaguchi, Masao (山口昌男). *Bunka to ryogisei* (『文化と両義性』[Culture and Ambiguity]). 1975. Tokyo: Iwanamishoten, 2000.

———. *Tennosei no bunkajinruigaku* (『天皇制の文化人類学』[The Cultural Anthropology of the Emperor System]). 1989. Tokyo: Iwanami-shoten, 2000.

Yoshida, Sanroku. "Kenzaburo Ōe: A New World of Imagination." *Comparative Literature Studies* 22.1 (1985): 80–96.

Index

About the Author

Akio Kimura received his M.A. from Sophia University (Tokyo, Japan) and his second M.A. and Ph.D. from Drew University (New Jersey, U.S.A.). He has published articles on William Faulkner, Oe Kenzaburo, James Baldwin, Katherine Anne Porter, and genocide. He is Associate Professor at Kanagawa University (Kanagawa, Japan).